I0796294

REMEMBER AND REHEARSE

J. T. ENGLISH

REMEMBER AND REHEARSE

AN INVITATION TO PARTICIPATE IN GOD'S STORY

Printed in the United States of America

979-8-3845-2094-8

Published by B&H Publishing Group
Brentwood, Tennessee

Dewey Decimal Classification: 220.07
Subject Heading: BIBLE—STUDY AND TEACHING / BIBLE—READING / BIBLE—USE

Cover design by B&H Publishing Group. Author photo by The Southern Baptist Theological Seminary staff.

1 2 3 4 5 6 7 • 28 27 26 25

To Macy, Thomas, and Bailey: I love learning how to live in God's story with you. Through all of it, let's keep pointing each other to the one who lives in God's story perfectly, Jesus Christ (Phil. 2:1–11).

Contents

CHAPTER 1 The Power of Stories 1

CHAPTER 2 False and Disorienting Stories 13

CHAPTER 3 The True Story 31

CHAPTER 4 Creation: The King Establishes His Kingdom 47

CHAPTER 5 Fall: Rebellion in the Kingdom 67

CHAPTER 6 Covenant with Abraham: The Kingdom Promised 85

CHAPTER 7 Covenant with Moses: The Kingdom Kept 103

CHAPTER 8 Covenant with David: The Kingdom Expected 121

CHAPTER 9 Covenant in Exile: The Kingdom in Darkness 135

CHAPTER 10 Christ: The Good News of the King and His Kingdom 151

CHAPTER 11 The Spirit and the Church: The King and His People 175

CHAPTER 12 Kingdom without End: The Coming of the King 201

About the Author 219
Acknowledgments 221
Notes 223

CHAPTER 1

The Power of Stories

Few things on earth rival the power of stories. Humans have always been captured by them. Whether ancient people in oral cultures handing down long and complex myths, a young child pretending to be the character of her favorite book, staying up late to finish a novel you can't put down, or watching the latest blockbuster at a movie theater, stories carry an unmatched power for influence.

We have always used stories to entertain, to inform, and to inspire, but they also hand down cultural values to the next generation, and they help us to make sense of the world. Stories do what no bullet-pointed list can do. They sneak past our defenses, powerfully moving our hearts and minds to respond not to cold propositions, but to a masterpiece that is interwoven with goodness, beauty, and truth when it is told well. And when we see these three, stories can command a deep sense of responsibility and action.

A person's story is the most personal thing they can share, wielding a power that helps us understand the storyteller in a way that photographs or show-and-tell never could. Whether we know someone or not, listening to their story shapes our understanding of who they are, how they've been shaped, and what their goals and dreams are, developing not simply knowledge, but deep empathy.

And what about your story? What story are you living? Stories not only help us understand others, they help us understand ourselves. We can't truly know ourselves unless we know what story we are living in. This story is not simply where do you live, who do you love, and what do you do. Your story is intertwined in a million ways with the stories of others, individual and communal. Every community you belong to has a story that gives its members a shared understanding of meaning and purpose. Shared stories bring a feeling of community founded on shared principles or promises. Think of these:

- If you join our gym, you'll be part of our family and you will live the good life of fitness and health.
- If you come to our university, you will be part of our community forever. You will

receive an education that will help you live the intellectual good life and earn a meaningful income.

- If you cheer for our team, you will be part of the family when we win the championship.
- If you come to our theme park, you will experience excitement, joy, and adventure.

Every community is telling a story and inviting you to be part of it.

But most of us don't wake up every day thinking about stories. We don't think about the story of the world. We don't think about other people's stories and we don't think about the story we're living in. We just live. Yet that doesn't mean stories are absent; it means they are so deeply ingrained in our lives that we don't even notice them.

Richard Kearney, professor of philosophy at Boston College, points out that "telling stories is as basic to human beings as eating. More so, in fact. For while food makes us live, stories are what makes our lives worth living."[1] Whoever tells the best story wins. Stories bring meaning, a prize for which all humans run.

For millennia, deep meaning has been found in shared stories, but in a world of fractured attention, individualism, and distraction, shared stories are all but lost. For many of us, it feels like the stories we thought we were living actually lack the meaning we thought they had. So much of the current moment that is shaped by anxiety, fear, and existential crisis can be traced back to a lack of shared true stories.

But it's not enough to simply recognize stories as powerful. We have to recognize that the power of stories can orient us to what is true, good, and beautiful. And if they have this power, they also have the power to disorient us from what is true, good, and beautiful. There are true stories and there are false stories. There are stories that can build up individuals and communities for a fruitful life and stories that will ravage individuals and communities, leading to their downfall and destruction.

As Alistair McIntyre argues, "I can only answer the question, 'What am I to do?' if I can answer the prior question of what story or stories do I find myself apart."[2] In other words, what you did or did not do today was largely a result of what story you perceive yourself to be living in.

Stories are the orienting feature of our lives. We don't just tell stories; we live in them. They draw our maps of reality, give us our internal compass, and set us along the road we have chosen to walk. Perhaps without even realizing it, we are living in a story that is helping us more deeply understand who God is, who we are, and what the world is—or we are living in a story that is pulling us away from those things. And the most persuasive stories are persuasive precisely because we don't realize they are stories. We just assume they are reality.

The Goal of This Book

Jesus was profoundly aware of the power of stories. He was often using stories and parables to help His disciples be reoriented to the kingdom of God. He used stories to shape and form the imagination of His disciples. He told the story of the persistent widow, the prodigal son, the unforgiving servant, the parable of the soils, and many others. Jesus understood that stories have a profound impact on us.

We are being discipled by stories. To be a disciple is to be a learner, and all of us are learning how to live in different stories. Stories are powerful teachers and we must be aware of what story or stories we are being taught and what story or stories we are living. If stories punctuate our lives, then to be a disciple of Jesus is to be "re-storied." Disciples of Jesus are in the process of having their stories re-scripted by the storyline of Scripture.

The goal of this book is very simple: it is an invitation to participate in the one true story of the world—the story of Scripture. In order to do that, two things will need to happen by the conclusion of this book.

First, you'll need to become more familiar with your story. Because most of us have never taken the time to examine ourselves, we're unaware of what story we're living in. So, before we can go too far forward, we have to go back—back to consider what stories have shaped us and informed our values and opinions and desires and fears and longings. Let me be clear: I don't want you to know your story for the sake of itself, but so that you can learn how to more deeply integrate your story with the storyline of Scripture.

John Calvin, the sixteenth-century Protestant Reformer, argued that there are two kinds of wisdom: "Nearly all wisdom we possess, that is to say, true and sound wisdom, consists of two parts: the knowledge of God and of ourselves."[3] We cannot know ourselves as we are without understanding our stories; and we cannot know ourselves as we were created to be without understanding how we fit into God's story.

One exercise I will ask you to complete is to learn how to tell your story. I want to invite you to consider how major events and turning points in your life have shaped who you are, what you believe, what motivates you, and the goals you're pursuing. Ultimately, when you learn what stories you are living in, you are able to understand how you've learned to make sense of life's complexities. In the process, you'll discover some false stories that have held power over your life. We'll discuss that much more in depth in the next chapter.

Second, I really want you to know the story of the Bible. I want you to be able to read it, enjoy it, and follow the flow of the narrative. So often we miss that the Bible is one story centering on the person and work of Christ. I want you to know the story well enough to be able to relay the story of Scripture to your kids, your spouse, your parents, or even your dog!

What I've found to be true over the course of my ministry is that people tend to be very good at remembering the *stories* of the Bible, but not quite as good at being able to rearticulate the *story* of the Bible. You might be familiar with the story of Noah, the story of the Exodus, the story of David, and the parable of the Good Samaritan, but you aren't quite sure how all of those stories fit together into the one story of Scripture. My hope is that this book will help with that.

Sometimes people are a little bit more familiar and are able to communicate simple overviews of the whole story of Scripture like "creation, fall, redemption, and consummation." While that is a faithful and helpful framework for understanding the story of the Bible, I want to press you to go a little bit further in this book. I want you to be able to tell the story of Scripture in a way that would captivate someone who has never heard it; to be able to tell the story of Scripture in a way that would capture the imaginations of the fourth graders you teach on Sunday mornings. I want you to be able to tell the story of the Bible to your grandchildren who are entirely unfamiliar with Scripture, and able to tell the story of the Bible to coworkers, neighbors, and college roommates who didn't grow up around the Christian faith and know nothing about it.

Most importantly, I want you to become so familiar with the story of Scripture—not just so that you can retell it, but so that you can learn to live in it. It is impossible to live in a story you don't know. I want you to become more familiar with the story of Scripture—not just so that you can look at it, but so that you can learn to be a participant so that it becomes the lens through which you view the rest of the world. I want the story of Scripture to become your interpretive framework for the entirety of your life.

Remember and Rehearse

A few weeks ago my wife and I celebrated our wedding anniversary. Every year since we've been married, we spend some time on our anniversary remembering not only the day of our wedding, but our dating history, the week leading up to our wedding, our rehearsal dinner, the wedding ceremony itself, and God's faithfulness to us all of these years since.

Each time, when we spend time remembering, it becomes easier to remember. Every year, the memories come rushing back in as if it happened yesterday: specific conversations with loved ones, specific details about the ceremony. We remember all that God has done over the decades since we met. It really feels like when we remember and rehearse that day, we are reliving it, able to remember it again the next time.

Similarly, the way we live the biblical story is by remembering and rehearsing it. However, we don't simply look at it as if it is just an event in the past to observe—we live it.

To re-member is put something back on, and when we remember the story of Scripture, we are putting on the storyline, intentionally looking back to who God is and all that He has done. We remind ourselves of God's faithfulness to His people.

But learning how to participate in the storyline of Scripture is not just about remembering; it's also about rehearsing.

Part of our wedding festivities so many years ago was also a rehearsal. We gathered together with everybody who would be part of our wedding ceremony the day before the wedding and rehearsed every single detail of the ceremony so that we could get it just right. We spent time rehearsing every little detail, so when the next day came, we'd be ready.

Part of participating in the storyline of Scripture is rehearsing events that have not yet taken place, making ourselves ready for what is to come. We are living within the storyline of Scripture—it is not yet completed. But there is a beautiful future kingdom that is coming for us; and as God's people, we are invited to rehearse God's future faithfulness to us. We are still living in the middle of the story with so much yet to come, rehearsing as we do for weddings, knowing the coming of this kingdom is sure.

- When we remember, we remind ourselves that the story of the Bible is ours to put on.
- When we rehearse, we invite ourselves into the future story of Scripture that is also ours.

When we remember, we put something back on. When we rehearse, we get ready for what's to come.

To become faithful participants in the storyline of the Bible, we both look back in remembrance and look forward in rehearsal. True remembrance is participation in the story of the past. True rehearsing is participation in the story of the future.

Summary

Human beings are shaped by stories. Our stories shape our imagination, our deepest hopes and longings, our fears and anxieties, the way we want to be treated, the way we treat other people, and what we think about God and life and reality. The goal of this book is to help you live in the true story.

Discussion Questions

1. What is one of your favorite stories? What about the story is powerful for you?

2. How would you tell the story of the Bible to someone else from beginning to end in ten minutes? Write your outline here or find a friend to practice with. (Don't let perfection get in the way; we're just looking for you to make progress. Let's see where you are starting.)

3. What areas of the Bible feel generally familiar? What feels more foreign or unknown?

CHAPTER 2

False and Disorienting Stories

Practice makes perfect. At least that's what my basketball coach used to tell me. I loved basketball so much that the hoop bolted to the front of our house eventually ripped the siding off. I had aspirations of being great, and my coach told me that with hard work, dedication, and practice, I could be as good as I wanted to be.

It is probably important for you to know that in high school I weighed about 145 pounds, soaking wet, stood around 5'10" tall, and was an average athlete at best. But still, I worked hard.

I was motivated. Driven. While practice made me a pretty decent player, more practice couldn't help me be as good as I wanted to be, as my coach had promised. I needed a miracle.

I'm thankful for a coach that motivated me, but I certainly believed the story he told me. Work hard and go far. While this story is powerful, it isn't always true. For me, no matter how hard I worked, high school basketball would be the furthest I could go.

Practice makes perfect is a powerful story, but it isn't always a true story.

Not all stories are created the same. While some orient us to truth, beauty, and goodness, others tend to disorient us from truth, beauty, and goodness. In a fallen and broken world, we all, to some degree, live in false and disorienting stories. We cannot avoid them. They come from our families and our experiences in life. They come from our favorite books and movies. Whether we know it or not, we have been deeply and profoundly shaped by various stories.

False Stories

Now, there are two tricky things about false stories. First: most of them are not 100 percent false or completely disorienting. False stories almost always hold some truth—and may even hold elements to be redeemed. But if these stories are lived wholeheartedly, they will ultimately lead us away from the one true story and the gospel. We have to learn to discern the truths from the half-truths amidst the disorienting narrative.

Every disorienting story overpromises and underdelivers.

Second, we're all participating in disorienting stories without being aware of it. That's why stories are so powerful. If you read the false stories below and only think about other people you know who are living in them, you'll really miss the point. As you read, turn the magnifying glass toward yourself. Examine your own heart. Prayerfully ask God to show you which false stories you're living in.

Ask yourself,

What purpose am I living toward?

What goals am I aiming at?

How do I make sense of the complexities of life?

You may see your answers to these questions in the descriptions below of disorienting stories you may find yourself living in. This is not an exhaustive list but it is a list of many common to our time. As you see yourself reflected in them, take note so that as you continue to read you can replace them with a better story.

Romanticism

This is the story that tells you, *You are your feelings.* Now, we're not talking necessarily about feelings we would call "romantic," though that may be relevant. Romanticism grew out of the eighteenth-century movement that prioritized feelings and the "inner self" over external realities. It tells you to be very in touch with how you feel. Not only are your feelings real, they are reliable and trustworthy. The more intensely you happen to feel any emotion, the more authentic that feeling is. If you live in the story of romanticism, you are always in search of deeper and deeper feelings to authentically express to the world. The good life is found in true authenticity.

Those of us who tend to live in the false story of romanticism can be swept away by a deep sense of feeling, reorienting our entire world around how we feel. We may also believe we must always affirm the "authentic" self-expression of other people, because they are just being "true to themselves." But this is a dangerous place to be! One of my friends gave me a helpful reminder once. He said, "Our feelings are real, but they are not always reliable." For those of us who struggle with the false story of romanticism, we tend to believe that our feelings are always reliable; we tend to always validate how others feel as true expressions of authenticity and reality; and we are driven by "feeling all the feels."

Consumerism

This story tells you, *You are what you have*. In this story your worth is based upon the value and quality of things that belong to you. For you, the good life is found in having, purchasing, consuming, and maintaining. This is the story that tells you happiness is found at the mall. True joy is found in clicking "add to cart" on your favorite website. Flourishing is found in always noticing and commenting on what other people have.

Struggling with the false story of consumerism doesn't always look like having the nicest things, but is characterized by finding comfort and security in having things. People who live in the story of consumerism tend to check their bank account daily, may have a hard time giving used things away, or may still have their kids' toys despite the fact that they are now all grown up. These things of life—the very things Jesus said would be destroyed by moth and rust—cannot provide what the person living this false story desires, making them accumulate more and more and more.

Rationalism

This is the story that tells you, *Whatever seems reasonable to you must be true.* You deeply trust your own ability to reason. You have a deep sense of distrust of emotions and potentially religious tradition as well. For you, the good life is found in using your mind as the arbiter of what is true and good. The primary way that you engage with people is by engaging with their ideas. For those who live in the story of rationalism, ideas are primary and feelings are secondary.

People who live in this story usually have the last word in arguments. They say things like, "I'm just looking at the facts." Again, as with all of these false stories, there is a profound sense of truth to rationalism. God made an ordered and rational world. Humans are rational creatures. However, people who live in the false story of rationalism are overly confident, maybe even prideful, in their own ability to be more reasonable than anybody else. It is a misplaced assumption that they can see the world more clearly than others.

Pragmatism

This is the story that tells you, *Whatever works must be true*. You find deep satisfaction in problem-solving, in making things work, and in efficiency. For you, the good life is found in productivity, functionality, and practicality. You love the phrase, "If it's not broken, don't fix it."

People who live in the false story of pragmatism love to make lists of goals, not necessarily because they want to accomplish the goal, but because they want to check something off. True happiness is finishing to-do lists. This story tells us to not ask the question, "Is it good?" but to rather ask, "Does it work?" Pragmatists don't want to bother with the question, "Did we do it right?" but want to ask, "Is it done?" For pragmatists, there is a deep pursuit of efficiency and accomplishing tasks, sometimes no matter what the task is.

Individualism

This story tells you, *You are at the center of all things.* Ultimately, the story you're living in is all about you. For you, the good life is found in autonomy and authority. You are the ultimate independent individual, the captain of your own destiny.

This story, at least in our day, overlaps a great deal with romanticism. People who live in the story of individualism can't conceive of any story that doesn't revolve around them. In particular, they can't conceive of any story that doesn't prioritize their feelings and authentic self-expression. They interpret all events through themselves: their desires and their wants. They have a hard time expressing empathy for other people or celebrating the victories of others because at the end of the day, it's all about them.

Hedonism

This story tells you, *Pleasure is at the center of a meaningful human experience.* If you find yourself inhabiting this story, you often seek out adventure and pleasure in everything you do. You don't bother with the question, "Is it right?" but rather ask, "Does it feel good?" You are afraid of being left out and your greatest desire is for your life to be an epic adventure. For you, the good life is found in pleasure.

People who live in this story desire to avoid suffering and sacrifice at all costs. They don't see any meaning or purpose in it because life is about what feels good. People who live in this story always have the next vacation planned. They always know the best place to eat. They often have a hard time curbing their sexual appetites—or may not even want to. And they are driven by always making the experience a little bit better. The primary ethic of hedonism is as long as nobody's getting hurt by this, what's the problem?

Progressivism

This story tells you, *Things are continually getting better.* You are regularly looking forward to advancements in science, technology, and economics, among others. You believe the human condition is constantly improving. For you, the good life is found in the belief that through human ingenuity and progress, we are going to be better today than we were yesterday, and better tomorrow than we were today.

While we should all be thankful for the development of penicillin and other advances in medicine and society, this false story creates an expectation that the world is getting better by itself. Progressivism is rooted in a very high view of human nature. People who tend to live in this story are surprised when wars break out. They are shocked when societies begin to unravel. They don't know how to understand when this story begins to erode under their feet, because for progressivism, things are constantly getting better.

Deconstructionism

This story tells you, *Institutions, traditions, and rituals that came before you should be viewed with skepticism and doubt.* You primarily view the world through the lens of power structures and believe that those with power in the past, present, and future should be viewed negatively because they are always oppressing others to feed their own desires. The primary contribution you believe you are making to the world is to tear down those traditions that came before you so that something better can be built in the future. For you, the good life is found in criticism and upending the status quo.

People who live in the story of deconstructionism are skeptical to the point of cynicism of anything that came before them, viewing everything that fits this bill as a potential tool of oppression, not meant to be conserved or preserved for coming generations, but to be torn down. Unfortunately, people who live in this story often see themselves as more righteous than anyone who came before them. They tend to believe the myth of "chronological snobbery"—*Nobody got it right before me, but thank goodness I am here to set everything right!*

Perfectionism

This story tells you, *You will not be loved until you are perfect and once you have made everything around you perfect.* You have an innate ability to walk into a room or a situation and see the things that are wrong or could be better. For you, the good life is found in finally correcting all of the mistakes about yourself and the world.

Lots of people live in the false story of perfectionism, and many of them are very religious. At the very core of their being, they want things to be perfect and right, especially within themselves. They have a deep sense of injustice about things that are not good. People who live in this story walk into a room—or look in a mirror—and only see flaws, often becoming highly critical of all the aspects of their life and even the lives of others.

Postmodernism

This is the story that tells you, ironically, *There is no big, overarching, true story.* In this story, all experiences, truth claims, and stories are equally valid. It is hard for you to believe there is any such thing as capital T Truth. For you, the good life is found in everyone's unique experiences, and to try to impose your story on another person is a form of oppression. To each his own! Truth is ultimately found in the subjective, in perspectives, and in experiences.

People who live in the false story of postmodernism are very skeptical of truth claims because, for them, truth is not found in external reality, but in the eye of the beholder. Objectivity is denied and subjectivity is preferred. Those who live in the postmodern story are uninterested in looking at things through any objective lens. Rather they desire to simply allow all experiences to be weighed equal.

Fatalism

The false story of fatalism tells you, *Things are perpetually getting worse.* In this story, it's easy to interpret all experiences as a downward spiral. Don't show these people WebMD, because they will inevitably think they're dying!

People who live in this story have usually been deeply hurt by the world. They have an ingrained sense of skepticism that things will not work out, that things are dark and only getting darker, and that someone or something is out to get them. This fatalistic perspective often creates a deeply embedded sense that it's only a matter of time before the next shoe drops. Until the next tragic phone call or the next inevitable crisis, those who live in the story of fatalism simply believe we should eat, drink, and be merry, because tomorrow we die.

Politicalism

The false story of politicalism tells you, *Everything will be right when human governments and politicians make them right.* If their preferred politician gets elected, they're elated; if not, they think the world is ending. Their mood swings drastically based on election results because they're putting all their hope and trust in people and parties. Christians who live in the false story of politicalism begin reading the book of Revelation or Daniel, believing they are undoubtedly living in the end times, when their favorite political party does not win the election.

People who live in this story often fail to realize what a small part of the world and a small moment in history they live in. They tend to associate their current nation with the kingdom of God—or the potential kingdom of God, believing this cultural moment is the most significant in human history without considering the many rises and falls that have come before and will come after them. The false story of politicalism convinces us that there is a one-to-one correlation between our political moment and the kingdom of God. They so easily forget that there is only one King and one kingdom that will last forever.

Safetyism

This story tells you, *The goal of life is safety in a dark and dangerous world.* You likely have as much insurance as you can afford and never let your kids out of your sight. For the person living the story of safetyism, there is no limit to the potential worst-case scenarios or to their preparation for them.

Safetyism tells people that they can create their own circumstantial safety that will help them avoid all negative consequences. Safetyism prepares for the worst so that it never happens. The good life is found in avoiding risk and pursuing safety.

Secularism

This story tells you, *There is nothing beyond what can be seen and experienced in the natural world.* This worldview believes in the possibility of exclusive humanism—that life can be lived without any reference to a divine being or transcendent experiences. Simply put, what you see is what you get, so make the best of it. For people who live in the narrative of secularism, the good life is found in shifting our attention away from any divine meaning and to earthly concerns of humanity, to flourishing, and to improving the human experience.

Is There a True Story?

So what story are you living? One, two, or many of these? Or is there a story God has brought to your mind that wasn't listed, but is just as pervasive in your heart?

These—and others—are the stories being told all around us. Every movie, every social media ad, every book, every consumer good, is telling a story that is competing for your heart and your attention. And it's very easy for us to begin living into parts of these stories without even realizing it. Most are very persuasive, because while they are false stories, not everything about them is false. As a matter of fact, not every, but almost every single one of these stories has redeemable features. The problem with these stories is when they become totalizing, when we make them ultimate and find our purpose and meaning within their storyline, often without even knowing it.

But there is a true and better story, a story that is simultaneously true, good, and beautiful in every way, orienting us so that we might also find these in our lives. There is a story that perfectly and authoritatively tells us who God is, who we are, what we are supposed to do, what He's doing in the world, and how we should respond to Him, and it is an invitation to find the good life in the only One who is good, the only One who can bear the weight of our expectations and hopes.

Because of the reality of sin—an unfortunate truth of the Christian story—we do not live in the Christian story by default. God's story is something we have to be born—or rather, reborn—into, and it's something we have to continually commit to and persevere in. One of the most essential elements for Christian disciples is not just realizing that we sometimes live in false stories, but that we must work, intentionally, on living in the true story.

In God's mercy, He has given us His Word, which is a story. Yes, there are lots of stories and glorious truths in Scripture, but all of those stories and all of those truths can only be rightly interpreted in the context of the far larger story of the Bible. This is the story of the sixty-six books of the Bible beginning in Genesis and ending in Revelation, which are all bound up in the person and work of Jesus Christ. The Bible is one unified story about Him, and as we read, we participate with Him. He is the perfect discipler—the teacher we all need—using this story to mold us into His image.

Christian discipleship is about living the biblical story, but you can't live in a story you don't know. Over the next several chapters, we are going to spend time looking at several of the major turning points in the Christian story so that you might know the One it reveals and live in His true and better story.

Summary

We are always being told stories. But most of those stories are false—or have enough truth to seem compelling, but enough falsehood to do a lot of damage. We are all, to some degree, living in false and disorienting stories, and we cannot grow in the true story unless we start to identify the false stories that have captured us.

Discussion Questions

1. Which false stories do you most identify with?

2. How do these false stories carry some truth? Where do they diverge from the truth we find in the Bible?

3. What other false stories have influence in your life?

4. How can the storyline of Scripture become a tool for you to combat the false stories of the world?

Formation Assignment: The Christian Story

Spend 20–30 minutes creatively remembering the story of your life. You may plot it on a timeline, make a list, or write it as a story. Include 10–15 significant turning points in your life. Identify the false story, or stories, you most identified with during different times in your life.

CHAPTER 3

The True Story

Have you ever heard someone use the phrase, "back in Bible times"? This phrase has always bothered me. I understand what people mean by it, but I want to yell out to them, *"We are still living in Bible times!"* The same God who interacted with His people way back then is continuing to invite participation in His story. The same Jesus Christ who the disciples saw rise up into heaven in order to take His rightful place on the throne is still reigning and ruling from there today. The same Holy Spirit who was poured out on the disciples at Pentecost is being poured out today by King Jesus as He builds His church.

The Bible is not a story from a long time ago and a galaxy far, far away. The Bible is a story about this world, and it is just as relevant today as it was all those years ago.

In the midst of innumerable false or disorienting stories, there is only one true story—the story told in the Bible. Maybe you've never thought of the Bible as one story, or perhaps you grew up thinking about the Bible as a list of rules to make you a good person. Maybe you were taught it is a collection of inspirational teachings or you've sought to use it as a systematic theology textbook. While the Bible can be used with some profit in these ways, it is first and foremost a story—one comprehensive narrative about what God has accomplished for sinners through the person and work of Jesus Christ.

You are living in a cosmic drama that started well before you were born, is continuing now in your life, and will continue on into eternity, all of which is found in this one, true, unified story. Scripture is not primarily a list of rules, though it does tell us what to do and what not to do. It is not a compilation of various teachings or even a textbook. It is a drama, and you are invited not to be a spectator, but to participate. This is discipleship: learning to follow Christ as a participant in this story.

The Bible is not only a story to be read; it is a story to be lived in. But to truly participate in this way, we must identify and remove the false stories we are living so that we can put on the better story. To grow as a disciple of Jesus is to have your story rescripted by His Spirit, edited to follow the contours of Scripture and written so that we may participate.

Yet, if we are meant to be participants in the Bible, we have to know the Bible. An actor playing a part cannot perform a script they don't know. Put simply, we can't live in the story of Scripture if we don't know the story of Scripture.

But sadly, many Christians are doing just that—trying to live a story they don't know. According to the 2022 state of theology research produced by Ligonier and Lifeway, evangelicals believe the following about the Bible:[4]

- Seventy-one percent agree with the following statement: Everyone is born innocent in the eyes of God.
- Fifty-three percent agree with the following statement: The Bible, like all sacred writings, contains helpful accounts of ancient myths but is not literally true.
- Fifty-six percent agree with the following statement: God accepts the worship of all religions, including Christianity, Judaism, and Islam.
- Thirty-eight percent agree with the following statement: Religious belief is a matter of personal opinion; it is not about objective truth.

Each of these beliefs betrays the true story of Scripture, revealing that evangelical Christians are living in other stories.

We are living in a moment as a church where we have never had more or easier access to our sacred text. But the reality is, we have not taken advantage of it. Our Bibles sit on the shelves; our preachers preach self-help mantras; and as a result, the church is forgetting the story that we have been called into.

Now, it may be easy to simply view that data and assume that it's not true about us or our church. So let's dig a little deeper. How would you answer the following questions?

- Can you tell the story of Scripture in fifteen minutes?
- Can you define the kingdom of God?
- What is a covenant?
- What are the major covenants found in Scripture and what do they promise?
- Where are they located in Scripture?
- How do the covenants help us know the full story?
- How do the covenants relate to Jesus and what He came to accomplish?

Bible literacy is one of the greatest challenges facing the modern church. But the goal of increasing the biblical literacy of the church is not that we would simply do better on Bible quizzes or have the right answer at Sunday school class. Bible literacy matters because biblical living is essential. The goal is not right answers, but a right life, participating in the great joy of fellowship with God. This book is going to help you tell the story of the Bible. It's going to help you answer these questions. It's going to help you identify one major theme that can be traced across the storyline of Scripture—the importance of biblical covenants, how they relate to each other, and where they are located; but most importantly, this book is going to show you how King Jesus is at the very center of the story of Scripture, and how He is the King who has come to fulfill His covenants. This book will grow the church's capacity to participate in the story of Scripture.

This chapter will serve as an introduction to Scripture's story. This is where we can get our bearings a little bit. Here we will look at some major categories that we will delve into much more deeply in upcoming chapters.

The Bible Is the True Story

You might be asking yourself, *Why should I trust that the story of the Bible is true?* That's a fair question. It is also a question that the Bible answers for itself.

Writing to Timothy, the apostle Paul explains the importance of Scripture in the Christian life. He says, "All Scripture is inspired by God and is profitable for teaching, for rebuking, for correcting, for training in righteousness, so that the man of God may be complete, equipped for every good work" (2 Tim. 3:16–17). When Paul tells Timothy that Scripture is "inspired," he's using a very important word, a word that is only used in one place in Scripture. *Inspired* means that the very words of Scripture are the very words of God. God is the author of the storyline of the Bible. The divine origin of Scripture does not in any way negate the human authorship of Scripture, but rather demonstrates to us that the Bible was written by God through human authorship in order to help all people know and love Him.

Similarly, Peter explains to us the divine and human nature of Scripture when he says, "Above all, you know this: No prophecy of Scripture comes from the prophet's own interpretation, because no prophecy ever came by the will of man; instead, men spoke from God as they were carried along by the Holy Spirit" (2 Pet. 1:20–21). This text reminds us that the Bible has a unique place in the Christian life as God's inspired, inerrant, authoritative, clear, and sufficient Word to help us follow Christ. It's impossible to follow Jesus without also being a student of Scripture.

A Kingdom-Shaped Story

The story of the Bible is the story of God establishing His kingdom on earth. While there are many important themes throughout Scripture—God's love, justice, redemption, reconciliation, presence, and more—Scripture reveals the kingdom of God as its most important theme. Once you begin to understand the narrative of the King and His kingdom, you will be equipped to see the storyline unfold in beautiful ways.

Perhaps this is a new idea for you, but it certainly was not new to Jesus or His disciples, or to the earliest readers of Scripture. The central theme of Jesus's teaching is this: "Repent because the kingdom of heaven has come near" (Matt. 3:2). The entire storyline of Scripture is an answer to this question: Is God going to establish His kingdom? This kingdom is described in the parables as a sower, a mustard seed, leaven, a hidden treasure, a costly pearl, a fishing net, new and old treasures. The teaching ministry of Jesus is about the kingdom.

Even after His death, burial, and resurrection, He is still teaching about the kingdom of God (Acts 1:3). Jesus's disciples, having seen His life, death, burial, and resurrection, could've asked the risen Christ anything.

> "What is it like to die?"
>
> "How did You rise from the dead?"
>
> "Can you tell us how you healed people?"

Did they ask Him any of this? No.

Instead, they asked Him, "Lord, are you restoring the kingdom to Israel at this time?" (Acts 1:6).

The kingdom is everything.

Don't miss this. These disciples could've asked Jesus anything, and they asked Him about the kingdom.

This question, perhaps more than any other, can help us become better readers and participants in the story of

Scripture. As you read the story of the Bible, you should be continually asking this question:

> "Has God's kingdom been finally, fully, and forever established?"

When you are reading any portion of Scripture, that is the question.

For Adam and Eve, the story of the Bible is about the kingdom.

For Abraham, the story of the Bible is about the kingdom.

For Moses, the story of the Bible is about the kingdom.

For David, the story of the Bible is about the kingdom.

For John the Baptist, the story of the Bible is about the kingdom.

For Jesus, the story of the Bible is about the kingdom.

For Jesus's disciples, the story of the Bible is about the kingdom.

The Old Testament is the story of the kingdom.

The New Testament is the story of the kingdom.

The Bible is all about the kingdom established, lost, promised, and re-established.

What Is the Kingdom?

But for some of us, the language of "kingdom" can feel strange, distant, and archaic. For some, it may even seem a little intense. *What is the kingdom, and what does it have to do with me?* That's why I want to provide a framework for us to begin to understand what the Bible means when it talks about the kingdom of God. While the framework is not exhaustive, it is certainly helpful if you want to be a better reader of Scripture.

The kingdom of God in Scripture can be understood through the lens of four P's: Presence, People, Place, and Purpose. They can be defined like this:

> **Presence:** God's presence with humanity in the world that He created. The story of the Bible is "God with us."
>
> **People**: The crowning achievement of God's creation is a people that will reign and rule with God as representatives on earth.
>
> **Place:** God's creation of the world and His gift of a location for His people to dwell and inhabit the kingdom of God in peace.
>
> **Purpose:** God's people living in accordance with the character, will, and covenants of God in the place that He has given them.

The kingdom of God is about God establishing His presence with His people in His place as they live out His purposes.

These categories can be enormously helpful to you as you read the Bible and seek to understand its big story. They can also be useful interpretive tools as you grapple with the meaning of a text.

As you read and seek to understand the big story of Scripture, you should be asking yourself some of these questions:

> Is God **present** with His people in this story? Of course God is omni-present—everywhere and always present—but are God's people experiencing the blessed presence of God in their midst? Or are they living in exile, searching for the presence of God?
>
> Are God's **people** reigning and ruling with God as His representatives or vice-regents, or are they establishing their own kingdom?
>
> Are God's people living in and enjoying the **place** that God has given to them as a gift to dwell and inhabit in peace?
>
> Are they living out the **purposes** of God found in His character, will, and covenants? Has God redeemed His people and granted them freedom from their sins?

The Kingdom Established (Gen. 1–2)
Presence: God creates a world and inhabits it by being present with His people (Gen. 1–2).
People: Humanity created by God as image-bearers and co-laborers (Gen. 1:26–28).
Place: God makes Eden for His people to enjoy and inhabit (Gen. 1:1).
Purpose: God's people representing God's glory to His creation (Gen. 1–2).

The Kingdom Lost and Reestablished (Gen. 3–Rev. 20)
Presence: God's people are cast away from His presence because of their sin (Gen. 3:22–24).
People: Our sinful rebellion makes us enemies of God in need of salvation (Gen. 3:15; Rom. 5).
Place: We live in exile, looking for and waiting for the kingdom of God (Gen. 3; 1 Pet. 1).
Purpose: Rather than represent God, we've become rebels in need of redemption and reconciliation (Rom. 1).

The Kingdom Coming (Rev. 21–22)
Presence: The dwelling place of God is with His people forever (Rev. 21:3).
People: We are declared to be God's people forever (Rev. 21:3).
Place: God gives His people a new kingdom to inhabit and the kingdom descends from heaven (Rev. 21:1–2).
Purpose: God's people enjoy the presence of the King forever (Rev. 21:22–24).

The story of the Bible is the story of this kingdom established in Eden, lost because of sin and rebellion, promised in the covenants, established through the person and work of Christ, waited for by the church, and fully consummated at the return of Christ. The story of Scripture, and the rest of this book, can be traced by following this simple outline. We will not attempt to exhaustively cover every portion of Scripture, but rather to specifically look at hot spots or major turning points in order to help the reader gain a better understanding of the structure for the narrative plot of the whole Bible. The primary turning points in Scripture are:

- Creation: Genesis 1–2
- Fall: Genesis 3
- Covenant with Abraham: Genesis 12–17
- Covenant with Moses: Genesis 19–24

BIBLICAL HISTORY TIMELINE

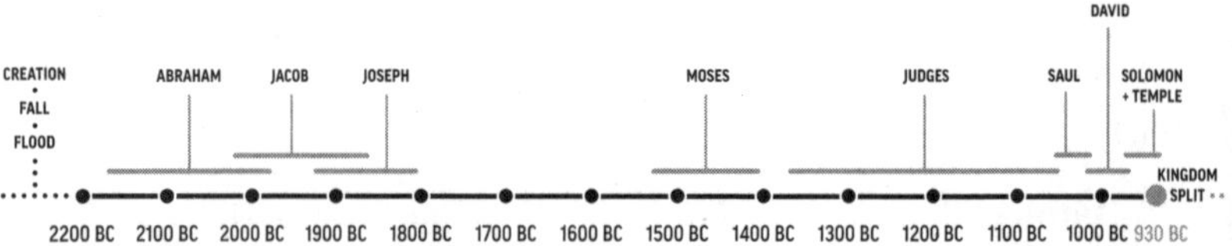

- Covenant with David: 2 Samuel 7
- Covenant in Exile: Jeremiah 31
- Christ: Matthew, Mark, Luke, John
- Church and Spirit: Acts 2
- Kingdom without End: Revelation 21–22

Again, the above outline is not exhaustive, but it does highlight the major turning points of the story of redemption. On the next page you will find a slightly more in-depth framework.

Every single movie, bedtime story, or epic drama follows a similar structure of exposition (introduction of characters), rising action (presentation of the problem), conflict (the problem confronted and defeated), falling action (what is happening now), resolution (the end). The world cannot help but follow the pattern of the one true story, so you'll find

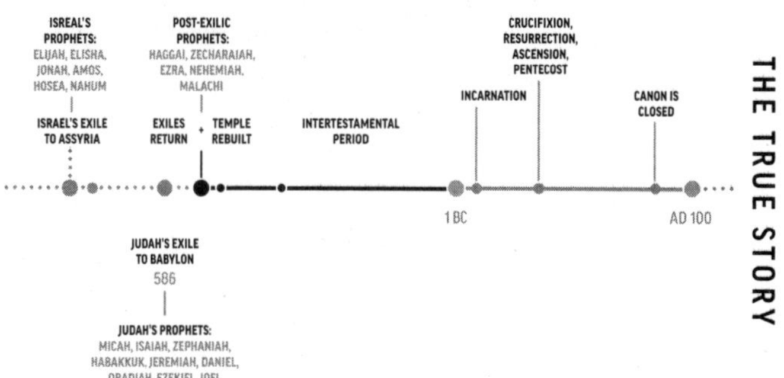

the structure familiar even if you are quite new to reading the Bible.

The false and disorienting stories of the world will lead your life toward chaos, destruction, and fear, but God is inviting you into a far better story—the story of His kingdom, a story that leads to life. He is not just inviting you to look at the story but to live in it, to participate in His kingdom.

Summary

The story of Scripture is the true story of the world that centers on the establishment of God's kingdom. The kingdom of God can be traced through four biblical themes: 1) God's presence; 2) God's people; 3) God's place; and 4) God's purposes.

Discussion Questions

1. As you think about the false stories you discovered in the previous chapter, how does the story of the kingdom of God help combat and confront them specifically?

2. How would you define the kingdom of God? What does it look like for you to participate in the kingdom of God?

3. What are some stories in the Bible that center on the presence or absence of God?

4. What does it mean to be God's people?

5. How would you define the place of God?

6. What purposes has God given His people?

Formation Exercise: The Christian Story

One of the goals of this book is to help you to be able to tell the story of Scripture conversationally over the course of 15–20 minutes, by using the framework of the kingdom of God—presence, people, purpose, and place. Practice again today using the above framework to guide you.

CHAPTER 4

Creation: The King Establishes His Kingdom

Beginnings matter. Classics are made in a strong first few lines, and books are quickly put down without being finished when those first lines are weak. Think of these famous first-liners:

> "It is a truth universally acknowledged, that a single man in possession of a good fortune, must be in want of a wife," from Jane Austen's *Pride and Prejudice.*
>
> "Call me Ishmael," from Herman Melville's *Moby Dick.*
>
> "It was the best of times, it was the worst of times, it was the age of wisdom, it was the

> age of foolishness, it was the epoch of belief, it was the epoch of incredulity, it was the season of Light, it was the season of Darkness, it was the spring of hope, it was the winter of despair," from Charles Dickens's *A Tale of Two Cities*.

These memorable opening lines introduce us to some of the world's most famous stories. An opening line is meant to make us curious, introducing major themes or key characters. The best introductions make bold statements, capture the reader's attention, and set the tone for the rest of the story. Ultimately, the beginning of a story is meant to invite the reader to become a participant in the story.

But none of these famous opening lines compares to the simple and bold statement that opens the narrative of Scripture:

> In the beginning God created the heavens and the earth. (Gen. 1:1)

This bold line sets out the entire framework for the story of the Scripture. From the very beginning the reader is told the Bible is about God. The story begins with Him, is sustained by Him, and is fulfilled by Him. The Bible begins with good news, "In the beginning, God."

The story of the Bible differs in almost every way from other origin stories, including our false stories. These often center on humanity, creation, many gods, or sometimes no gods, but the biblical account is different. The Bible doesn't give an account of multiple gods (polytheism). The Bible does not begin with humanity (perfectionism, pragmatism, romanticism, or secularism). The Bible does not begin with creation (materialism or consumerism). The Bible does not begin with God's absence (atheism or agnosticism). The Bible begins with the one true God—God the Father, God the Son, and God the Holy Spirit—eternally existing in peaceful and loving harmony, speaking all things into existence by the word of His power.

If the Bible begins with God, the rest of the story must be about God. This simple phrase helps us learn so much about Him. God was in the beginning and existed before the beginning. That means no one else existed besides Him; He alone has existed forever. God is the creator; everything else is His creation. He is self-existent, entirely independent from His creation. He is transcendent, existing above His creation. God is immanent, desiring to be with His creation. The Bible is about God, and that is good news.

This good news is not centered on creation—every false story centers on humanity—but this true and wonderful story is not about you. Yes, we are invited to participate in the storyline of Scripture, but that doesn't mean we are the central character. And this too is good news, because being the center of this cosmic story is a weight only God can carry. Scripture rightly places God at the center of the story, from the first bold, powerful line.

But the Bible does not just begin with a statement about God's existence. It includes a statement about His activity. "In the beginning God *created* the heavens and the earth" (Gen. 1:1, emphasis mine). God does not just simply exist. God acts. And His first activity in the biblical story is to establish His creation, where He will receive honor, glory, and praise.

It is really important that we see this. Genesis 1 does not hold a story of a king defeating another kingdom in order to claim it as his own. This is a story of a King speaking a kingdom into existence. The Christian story begins with a King establishing His kingdom.

The Kingdom Established

Genesis 1 gives a transcendent view of the establishment of the kingdom. The first three days describe how God creates different spaces. On the first day He creates the light and the darkness. On the second day He creates the sky and the sea. On the third day He creates the land. Then on the next three days God fills those spaces. On day four He creates the sun, the moon, and the stars. On the fifth day He creates the birds and the fish. On the sixth day He creates the animals and image-bearers. God forms and fills His kingdom.

Genesis 2 details a more immanent and intimate perspective of God's creation of His kingdom. He forms the man out of the dust of the ground by breathing life into him. He places the man in the garden in order to work and watch over it while also naming the animals and cultivating the garden. We learn that the man has no corresponding helper for him, so the Lord creates Adam's intimate ally, Eve.

In the establishment of the kingdom:

- God is **present** with His creation.
- God creates a **people** that belong to Him.
- God creates a **place** for His people to dwell.
- God gives His people the **purpose** of being His representatives to all of His creation.

God is present with His creation.

At the very heart of the story of Scripture is God's presence with His people. God is the *with-us* God. At the very beginning, God is present with His creation.

Genesis 1:2 says, "Now the earth was formless and empty, darkness covered the surface of the watery depths, and the Spirit of God was hovering over the surface of the waters."

This one little verse corrects two false stories: God is neither distant from His creation, withdrawing after creation, nor can it be said God is the creation. He is inextricably linked with the natural world—the animals and plants, the planets and stars as its creator and sustainer—but also wonderfully different from it. And God is *with* His creation.

Two categories that can help us understand God's presence with His creation are *transcendence* and *immanence*. The Bible presents a unique perspective as it relates to God's presence in and with His creation. Scripture emphasizes God's transcendence over His creation and His immanence with His creation.

God's transcendence refers to the distinction between God and His creation. To transcend means to be above and beyond something. God is the eternal, uncreated, self-existent creator of all things. He is above and beyond what He has created—all else pales in comparison to Him. Isaiah 66:1 nicely sums up God's transcendence: "Heaven is my throne, and earth is my footstool. Where could you possibly build a house for me?"

But God is not transcendent to the point of being distant from His creation. He is also immanent; God is near to His creation. Though God is above and beyond, He acts within and with His creation. He is transcendent, yet He stoops down low to relate to what He has created. Psalm 113 shows us God's careful attention to the world He has created—even the smallest and seemingly most insignificant things: "Who is like the Lord our God—the one enthroned on high, who stoops down to look on the heavens and the earth? He raises the poor from the dust and lifts the needy from the trash heap in order to seat them with nobles—with the nobles of his people" (vv. 5–8).

God is perfectly transcendent *and* perfectly immanent. He is the God who reigns over everything. He is the God who is near to that over which He reigns.

To put it in kingdom terms: The King reigns over His kingdom and He is the ever-present King.

Craig Bartholomew and Michael Goheen argue, "God is not a monarch who rules from afar and takes no interest in his territories or subjects. Having built his kingdom, God reigns over it in a deeply personal way."[5] From the opening pages of Scripture, the King reigns and the King is ever-present.

In Genesis 2 we continue to see the intimacy with which the king interacts with His creation. In this account the Lord is personal and near, specifically in His creation of the man. With no one to work and watch over the garden, the Lord "formed the man out of the dust from the ground and breathed the breath of life into his nostrils, and the man became a living being" (Gen. 2:7). In the garden of Eden we even see that the Lord God walks among His people at the time of the evening breeze (3:8).

From the beginning, we see that God is *with us* (Matt. 1:23). And this is a theme we will see repeated throughout the storyline of the Bible.

This means the goal of your life—and the goal of all creation—is to enjoy the presence of God.

Let me say that again. *The goal of your life is to enjoy the presence of God.*

All the happiness you're searching for, all the significance, all the meaning and purpose, all the joy and satisfaction—all of it is found in God's presence. "How happy is the one you choose and bring near to live in your courts! We will be satisfied with the goodness of your house, the holiness of your temple" (Ps. 65:4).

Life is found in God's presence. The goal of every human story should be finding rest in the presence of God.

This is how the story begins. The King reigns over and resides in the kingdom. That is good news.

God creates a people that belong to Him.

But God is not simply present with His creation. More specifically, He is present with His people. Genesis 1:26–27 explains this vision for humanity: "Let us make man in our image, according to our likeness. They will rule the fish of the sea, the birds of the sky, the livestock, the whole earth, and the creatures that crawl on the earth. So God created man in his own image; he created him in the image of God; he created them male and female."

There are two really important concepts in this passage: 1) Image-bearing and 2) the cultural mandate. The first relates to who we are and the second to what we are to do. As Jen Wilkin points out, "For the believer wanting to know God's will for her life, the first question to pose is not "What should I do?" but "Who should I be?"[6] We will discuss that purpose later in this chapter. Let's first turn to what it means to be who we are and then what we were made to do.

Theologians have long debated specifically what it means to be made in the image of God, but at its heart, the concept is fairly simple. It means that humanity is meant to be a reflection or a mirror of the One we represent. This certainly relates to what we were supposed to go do, but it also has significance for who we are. To be made in the image of God is to be endowed with inherent dignity, value, and worth, not because of what we do, but primarily because of the One who made us. Every human has dignity because every human belongs to God.

We are not like the rest of creation. Only humans have been made in the image of the King. And as His image-bearers, God's royal representatives share in the reign and rule of the one who made them.

It is hard to overstate the significance of the claim the Bible is making. When Moses penned those words, God's people were familiar with the language of image-bearing from their time in Egypt. Other cultures used this language to refer to royalty—individual kings and queens lauded as being in God's image because only they were able to represent their gods. In the ancient world, most societies and cultures reserved image-bearing language primarily or solely for the king.

What the world sought to individualize, the biblical account seeks to democratize. Dignity is not reserved for the few, but is extended to all. Royal authority and vocation are extended to every single image-bearer.

God creates both male and female in His image, distinguishing between the man and the woman, but He also proclaims that both are made in His image. In this passage, as well as in Genesis 2, we learn that not only was humanity made for God, but men and women were made for fellowship with each other. God's people are made for relationships.

This becomes even more clear in Genesis 2. In this creation account we are given a slightly different, but complementary perspective, on God's creation of image-bearers. God makes the male image-bearer, Adam, first. As the man begins exercising kingly rule over the kingdom, we read, "It is not good for the man to be alone. I will make a helper corresponding to him" (v. 18). God authorizes the man to take dominion by naming all of the animals, and he did, but no helper was found among them (v. 20). So God mercifully provides exactly what he needs. Genesis 2:21–22 says, "So the Lord God caused a deep sleep to come over the man, and he slept. God took one of his ribs and closed the flesh at that place. Then the Lord God made the rib He had taken from the man into a woman and brought her to the man." This is an act of God's divine mercy. In the creation of men and women, God has made two corresponding partners to bring Him glory.

Adam is well aware of his need for help when he responds to meeting his royal ally. When he sees her, Adam proclaims, "This one, at last, is bone of my bone and flesh of my flesh; this one will be called 'woman,' for she was taken from man" (v. 23).

The story is inviting us to affirm that both men and women share something in common—they are made in the image of God. Both men and women are image-bearers and endowed with divine authority to reign and rule over God's creation. It also invites us to affirm that men and women are distinct from each other and that they need each other in the mission that God is setting before them. This places great dignity on every human as those created in His image, and the dehumanization of any image-bearer is an attack on God's good design.

In order to know what role you play in the storyline of the Bible, you must understand who you are. We can't know what to do until we've established who we are. We are image-bearers, God's royal people.

We are not authors of our own story. We don't write our own scripts. As image-bearers we are written into God's script. Our identities are not achieved, but received—which removes a massive weight from our shoulders. God's people are made in His image and are invited to be participants in His kingdom.

God grants His people a place to dwell.

Sometimes we may think God does not care about physical things. After all, God is more interested in spiritual things, right? I encounter this belief a lot. Somewhere along the way so many of us were taught that God is more concerned with spirituality than He is physicality. But according to His Word, God cares about both!

I want to clear up two misconceptions that people often have about God's creation. We can call these two false beliefs *materialism* and *gnosticism*.

Materialism emphasizes the physicality of God's creation to the neglect or outright denial of spiritual reality. This worldview seeks to understand the world only as it relates to its physical parts.

Gnosticism emphasizes the spirituality of God's creation to the neglect of the physicality of God's creation. This worldview teaches that the material realm is inherently bad, and that salvation is a sort of escape from our bodies.

But the biblical story corrects both of these errors. The place God creates for His people equally emphasizes the physicality and the spirituality of His kingdom. The garden of Eden is where heaven and earth meet. The kingdom is physical and spiritual.

God cares about all aspects of His creation. God cares deeply about the place He made for His people.

A consistent theme in Genesis 1 is the repetition that God's creation is good. God created the light. *It was good.* God saw the dry land and the sea. *It was good.* God created plants that bear fruit. *It was good.* God created great lights for the sky. *It was good.* God created all living creatures. *It was good.* God created image-bearers. *It was good.*

Our response to God's creation should mirror Genesis 1:31, "God saw all that he made, and it was very good indeed." The king has established a place for His kingdom, and it is good! We were never meant to be nomads. At the heart of our story, we were not meant to be sojourners or exiles. Humanity has a home.

The place of God is where the people of God encounter the presence of God. The story opens with the distinct hope that God dwells on earth with His people. The garden of

Eden is the place where God intends for His people to dwell so that He might be present with them forever.

God's Purpose for His People

Our identity as the people of God translates to our purpose as the people of God. We are now God's royal representatives. This is often referred to as the *cultural mandate.*

Immediately after God created Adam and Eve in His image, Genesis 1:28 says, "God blessed them, and God said to them, 'Be fruitful, multiply, fill the earth, and subdue it. Rule the fish of the sea, the birds of the sky, and every creature that crawls on the earth.'" At the heart of the King's plan for the kingdom is the purpose that His image-bearers would rule over His kingdom as His royal representatives.

Humanity's purpose is to give glory to God as His representatives and royal image-bearers.

Humanity has not been given the authority to do whatever we want with God's creation. We are meant to be stewards, caretakers, and ambassadors for the King who presides over His kingdom. No other creature in God's kingdom has been commissioned in the same way God commissions humanity. We have been given a unique vocation and a holy calling in that we have been commissioned by God Himself to rule over the kingdom.

Central to the purpose of God's people is the expansion of the kingdom of God. As Adam and Eve began to rule over and subdue the earth, they were meant to extend the boundaries of the kingdom to all creation. They aren't meant to sit idly in the garden of Eden enjoying paradise; they are called to kingdom work. Humanity is meant to cultivate the garden of Eden and extend God's dominion and authority to all of creation.

Specifically, humanity is instructed to be fruitful and multiply in order to fill the earth (Gen. 1:28). This gives us a picture of an ever-growing population of royal representatives who will eventually fill the earth for the glory of God.[7]

As they fill the earth with God's royal image, they are also given the divine right to extend dominion and authority over everything that God has made. The Bible makes clear that one of the primary vocations of humanity is to work and keep the ground that God has graciously given them (Gen. 2:15). "The male and female as king and queen of creation are to exercise rule over their dominion, the extent to which is the entire earth," argues Stephen Dempster.[8] As image-bearers, they represent God by bringing order to chaos and by making broken things beautiful.

Our role as image-bearers is best understood as a royal stewardship. As God's ambassadors, our purpose is to serve, develop, and indwell God's creation in such a way that it is enhanced and God is glorified.[9]

From the very beginning of Scripture, humanity has been endowed and commissioned with a holy calling and purpose. We were made to work for the glory of God and His kingdom.

God's Kingdom Established

As we conclude the first two chapters of Scripture, one thing is clear: God's kingdom has been definitively established.

These categories will be instructive for us as we move through the story of Scripture and the kingdom of God.

- The king is **present** with His creation.
- The king creates a **people** that belong to Him.
- The king creates a **place** for His people to dwell.
- The king gives His people a **purpose** of being His representatives to all of His creation.

Remember and Rehearse

Remember that the story of the Bible is all about the establishment of God's kingdom.

The true story of the world revolves around the establishment of God's kingdom in all His creation. Our false stories often invite us into believing that life is all about establishing our own kingdoms, building something great for ourselves, or that the purpose of our lives is in leaving a legacy for our own glory. Remember, the Bible begins and ends with the establishment of God's kingdom and you are called to be a participant.

Remember that you are not God and you were never meant to be.

The establishment of God's kingdom in creation helps us remember God is the Creator, we are not. All too often our false and disorienting stories invite us to play God in our own narratives. We truly believe we are the center of the story, that we are in control, and that it's all about us, but at the very heart of the Christian story is the good news that God is God and you and I are not.

Rehearse the good news that you, and every other human, are made in the image of God.

We are also invited to rehearse so many beautiful truths in the establishment of the kingdom. We can rehearse the truth that all people are made in the image of God and full of dignity, value, and worth. That means that differences in socioeconomic status, gender, race, ethnicity, age, intellectual ability, or any other distinguishing feature may never be used to discriminate against another human being. To do so is to enact violence against a person made in the image of God and is an attack on God's kingdom plan itself. It also means you are not what you do—your value is not found in your work or what you are able to produce. It is not the work of your hands but the work of His that gives you value. You do not achieve value, you receive it. Rehearsing this truth is to live with loving care for those created in the image of God.

Rehearse the good news that your work has purpose.

Work is not simply a post-fall curse, but a pre-fall commissioning. You were made for a purpose, and as your false story is being re-scripted, your purpose is meant to be inextricably intertwined with the kingdom purposes of God. Your work is not meaningless. You are not just supposed to make some money and then spend it on whatever you want for pleasure. On the other hand, your work is not for you. Perhaps in your false story, work has become an idol. You are not meant to work in order to build a kingdom for yourself.

Your work matters because the glory of God matters. Rehearse this truth by working as unto the Lord, cultivating fruit in whatever you do for His glory.

God sees almost all vocations as a ministry. God does not desire for all of His people to be pastors, ministers, and missionaries—though He does call some to that work. Instead, it means God calls all people to be His representatives. You have the opportunity to represent God in your role as a mom or a dad, as a lawyer who works for justice, as a physician who works to bring healing, as an author who writes about truth, or as a creator who cultivates beauty. God is glorified when we represent Him in all domains of life.

Rehearse the good news that you were created to enjoy the presence of God.

The goal of every single human life is to enjoy the presence of God forever. When you practice spiritual disciplines that attune your attention to the God who made you, you are living toward God's ultimate purpose for you. How are you cultivating attention to God's presence in your life?

Summary

The story of the Bible begins with the establishment of God's kingdom. The King is **present** with His **people** in the **place** He has given them to live out His **purposes**.

Discussion Questions

1. How would you tell the story of the establishment of God's kingdom in creation?

2. How is the beginning of the Christian story different from other origin stories? Why is the Christian story better?

3. Compare and contrast the story of God's kingdom established with your false story.

4. What does it mean to be created in the image of God?

5. What is the "cultural mandate" and how does it apply to the kind of work God has given you?

CHAPTER 5

Fall: Rebellion in the Kingdom

There is no such thing as a good story without a tragedy. Every good story has some kind of crisis or conflict, a moment when the narrative takes an unexpected twist or turn for the worse. *Romeo and Juliet* begins with romance and ends with death. *Of Mice and Men* begins with aspiration and dreams but navigates challenges and tragedy. We are captivated by tragic stories because they often remind us of our own lives. The human experience is filled with twists and turns, conflict, challenges, and tragedy.

Life is riddled with pain, suffering, and heartache. The false stories we find ourselves living in are cheap coping mechanisms for trying to avoid the reality we all know: *something is wrong with us and something is wrong with the world.*

But why? How did things get this way? If God created the world to be His kingdom, why does it not feel that way?

God's world is created good. In this good world, God gives His people a law, and if they break that law, there will be dire consequences. We learn in Genesis 2:15–17,

> The Lord God took the man and placed him in the garden of Eden to work it and watch over it. And the Lord God commanded the man, "You are free to eat from any tree of the garden, but you must not eat from the tree of the knowledge of good and evil, for on the day you eat from it, you will certainly die."

You can't miss this. If humanity rebels against God's command, the consequences are tragic. We will die.

Now, I want you to read the opening lines from Genesis 3 slowly as if you've never read this text before:

> Now the serpent was the most cunning of all the wild animals that the Lord God had made. He said to the woman, "Did God really say, 'You can't eat from any tree in the garden'?"
>
> The woman said to the serpent, "We may eat the fruit from the trees in the garden. But about the fruit of the tree in the middle

> of the garden, God said, 'You must not eat it or touch it, or you will die.'"
>
> "No! You will certainly not die," the serpent said to the woman. "In fact, God knows that when you eat it your eyes will be opened and you will be like God, knowing good and evil." The woman saw that the tree was good for food and delightful to look at, and that it was desirable for obtaining wisdom. So she took some of its fruit and ate it; she also gave some to her husband, who was with her, and he ate it. Then the eyes of both of them were opened, and they knew they were naked; so they sewed fig leaves together and made coverings for themselves.

In just a few sentences we read the most tragic story ever told. Genesis 3:1–7 is less about what is wrong with the world and more about what *went* wrong—why we and the world are so broken and full of sin.

In Genesis 3 we find the birth narrative of death. Here we find the origin story for every cancer diagnosis, every natural disaster, every mental illness, every fractured family, every deception, and every broken relationship. It is not an exaggeration to say that every tragedy that has ever happened in the history of the world can be traced back to the first sin in the garden of Eden.

In Genesis 3 we see the kingdom of God lost.

- Depravity and death for the **people** of God
- Exile from the **presence** of God
- Groaning for the **place** of God
- Consequences for the **purposes** of God

Depravity and Death for the People of God

In Genesis 3, we see the ultimate reversal as it relates to God's people.

We were made to be representatives (Gen. 1:26), but now we are rebels.

We were formed out of the dust (Gen. 2:7), but now we return to the dust.

Because of our rebellion, there are just consequences for God's people. Disobedience results in death (Rom. 6:23).

As a result of Adam and Eve's rebellion, we are sinners by nature, this is known as total depravity. After the fall, humanity's nature is fundamentally changed. We didn't just make a bad decision; our very nature is now marked by brokenness and corruption. In God's original design we were granted a nature that was inclined to give Him glory. But now that we have rebelled against God, we have a nature inclined to give ourselves glory.

Instead of our souls bending up to God, they now bend in on themselves. The original sin of Adam and Eve has fractured and distorted every single one of us. Our innermost selves are turned inside out—fundamentally inclined not toward God but away from Him.

Those of us who prize radical individualism and personal autonomy may be inclined to think that Adam and Eve should suffer the consequences of their own sin. Why should their disobedience affect the rest of us?

It's a good question. The Bible describes a kind of headship and participation in Adam and Eve that incorporates all of us. In some sense, every single human is *with* or *in* Adam and Eve, and we all participated in this original sin. The apostle Paul explains the spiritual state of all of humanity when he argues, "just as sin entered the world through one man, and death through sin, in this way death spread to all people, because all sinned" (Rom. 5:12). This original sin is the first spiritual contagion that spread to every single one of us.

We see another dramatic reversal in this just consequence of our disobedience. The creation narrative of Adam tells us that he is taken up out of the dust and formed by God. As God intimately shapes and forms the first image-bearer, the breath of life is breathed into him (Gen. 2:7).

But Genesis 3:19 describes the physical consequence of our sin in this way, "You will eat bread by the sweat of your brow until you return to the ground, since you were taken from it. For you are dust, and you will return to dust." As a part of the consequences of our disobedience, we are no longer taken up from the dust and formed into the image of God. Instead, we return to the very dust and dirt from which we were formed.

We are meant to feel the stark imagery here.

CREATION:
Humanity formed from the dust and given the breath of life.

DEATH:
Humanity put back into the dust as we breathe our last breath.

Formed from the dust for *life*. Returned to the dust in *death*.

This is a de-creation narrative. The King's purposes have been thwarted. The very image-bearers who were formed by

God from the dust of the ground will return to that very same dirt as a result of their sin.

It is important that we understand the biblical imagery here. I often hear people talk about death in positive terms, and there is a sense in which I can understand what they mean. Often, the suffering that we endure in life can be so great that we are looking forward to being spiritually present with Jesus. However, we must recognize that death is not salvation; resurrection is. Humanity is meant to be taken up out of the ground, not put back into it.

The prophet Isaiah helps us understand death as a great enemy when he explains,

> On this mountain, the Lord of Armies will prepare for all the peoples a feast of choice meat, a feast with aged wine, prime cuts of choice meat, fine vintage wine. On this mountain he will swallow up the burial shroud, the shroud over all the peoples, the sheet covering all the nations. When he has swallowed up death once and for all, the Lord God will wipe away the tears from every face and remove his people's disgrace from the whole earth, for the Lord has spoken. (Isa. 25:6–8)

Our greatest hope is not in death. Our greatest hope is in the death of death.

Exile from the Presence of God

Immediately after Adam and Eve's rebellion we read, "Then the man and his wife heard the sound of the LORD God walking in the garden at the time of the evening breeze, and they hid from the LORD God among the trees of the garden" (Gen. 3:8). Created to enjoy the presence of God, they are now hiding from Him. Sin makes us avoid the very presence we were made to enjoy. While Adam and Eve should've run into the presence of God, asking for mercy, they are now scared, alone, and experiencing the shame of their rebellion.

Outside of a divine act of grace, this is now our lot. We hide. We cower. We try to avoid the presence we were made for. We intentionally deprive ourselves of intimacy with God. We refuse to come clean about our rebellion and instead we take cover behind fig leaves—anything and everything we can find to cover up our shame.

In the midst of our hiding, God asks Adam one of the most penetrating questions in Scripture. *"Where are you?"* (Gen. 3:9, emphasis mine).

This is not meant to indicate that God does not know where Adam is. He does. He's asking Adam if Adam knows where he is.

In an age that is obsessed with the question, "Who am I?" Maybe the better question is, "Where are you?"

Genesis 3 concludes with the chilling declaration that the very purpose for which we were created—to live in God's kingdom and enjoy the presence of the King—is removed from us, at least temporarily. Instead of being present with the King in the kingdom, we are sent into exile.

Genesis 3 explains,

> The Lord God said, "Since the man has become like one of us, knowing good and evil, he must not reach out, take from the tree of life, eat, and live forever." So the Lord God sent him away from the garden of Eden to work the ground from which he was taken. He drove the man out and stationed the cherubim and the flaming, whirling sword east of the garden of Eden to guard the way to the tree of life. (vv. 22–24)

Read these phrases again:

> So the Lord God sent him away.
>
> He drove the man out.
>
> The King has sent us away. We have been driven out.

Exile now characterizes the human experience. Exile is the loss of the presence of God. It is marked by pain and suffering. We know we have a home, but we don't know the way back. Exile is marked by a profound sense of deep loss and longing because we are also aware—under the surface—that our exile stems from our rebellion. Our exile is the result of our sin.

Exile is that deep existential sense, that groaning, that we have a home that we were made for, but we aren't currently there.

It is hard to imagine a more devastating fate than humans living outside the blessed presence of God. The most devastating result of the fall is not that we lost paradise, but that we lost God's presence.

Exile is a continual theme throughout the storyline of Scripture. Exile marks the stories of Abraham, Isaac, and Jacob, God's people in Egypt, Israel sojourning in the wilderness, Judah in Babylon, and the church living as sojourners and strangers in the world. God's people are enduring an almost unbearable exile as we watch and wait for the appearing of the King and His kingdom.

Groaning for the Place of God

When Adam and Eve sinned against God, humanity did not just lose His presence, we also lost the very place in which we were supposed to dwell with Him forever—Eden.

This is often overlooked in our highly transient society. We are living in a cultural moment where place has become unimportant to us. We move freely from neighborhood to neighborhood and nation to nation. A job might take us from one place to another. We might move to get away from family or to be closer to family.

But this freedom to come and go as we please has come at a great cost—it has cost us an important feature of what it means to be human: connection to a place.

We tend to overlook the profound impact that place is meant to have on us. Since the creation of the world, human identity has been deeply bound up with where we live, our place. At the heart of the consequences found in Genesis 3, is displacement from our home.

Not only that, but our relationship with the land given to us is now not one of harmony, but of intense labor. The ground from which we were made and that we are intended to cultivate is now cursed (Gen. 3:17). The place that was once paradise is now marked with thorns and thistles (v. 18).

Consequences for the Purposes of God

There weren't only consequences in the place of God, but also in the purposes of God for His people. In Genesis 1–2, the people of God are created to live out the purposes of God. More specifically, that purpose is to be fruitful and multiply, to represent God to the ends of the earth, and to cultivate His garden-kingdom to the ends of the earth by subduing all of creation. But this, too, changes after the fall.

Inherent in God's original design is humanity's fruitfulness and multiplication through procreation. But now, as a result of our rebellion, fruitful multiplication is painful. Specifically, the consequences God gives to the woman are, "I will intensify your labor pains, you will bear children with painful effort. Your desire will be for your husband, yet he will rule over you" (Gen. 3:16).

Similarly, the purposes for the man come under judgment when we are told, "The ground is cursed because of you. You will eat from it by means of painful labor all the days of your life. It will produce thorns and thistles for you, and you will eat the plants of the field. You will eat bread by the sweat of your brow" (3:17b–19a). The kingdom, which was once a gorgeous and nutritious garden, is now producing thorns and thistles. The gardener, Adam, who was created to work the land in joy and harmony, is now gathering his meals through fatigue and striving.

The very purposes for which we were created are now under the just consequences of judgment.

The result of our rebellion is the loss of God's kingdom. Our sinfulness has dire consequences for the presence of God, the people of God, the place of God, and the purpose of God.

The Promise of Hope

Just when it appears all has been lost, God demonstrates to His people that He is rich in mercy, despite the fact that His people now live in exile, enduring the consequences of their sin. He offers them some amazing news. This news comes in the form of a curse directed at the serpent—the snake who tempted Eve and Adam: "I will put hostility between you and the woman, and between your offspring and her offspring. He will strike your head, and you will strike his heel" (Gen. 3:15).

God's people are going to suffer the consequences for their disobedience, but we also see that one day God will deliver us.

Some theologians call this the first gospel. While God's people have a real enemy in the serpent, God promises to provide an offspring who will crush and destroy him forever.

One day, God promises, there will be a son born of the woman who comes to crush the head of the serpent. When we look to the womb of the woman, we see the consequences of our rebellion, but we also see the covenant promises of God.

Life East of Eden and the Kingdom of Babel

This promise of salvation is something God's people were looking for from the first moment they stepped outside the kingdom and began living east of Eden. God's people were always looking to the womb of the woman wondering, "Will this be the son to bring salvation?"

But life east of Eden is brutally painful. We can see the story of humanity in Genesis 4–11 as a series of ongoing tragedies as humanity continues to spiral further into chaos.

Even as we begin Genesis 4, we see that the man and the woman have two sons, Cain and Abel (Gen. 4:1). This seems like a positive turn of events. Eve is the mother of all living, and we can't help but wonder, is one of these sons the promised one who will restore the kingdom of God? Unfortunately, we read that one of the brothers, Cain, murders the other brother, Abel (v. 8).

Life outside the kingdom is marked by depravity and death.

Eventually a character emerges, Noah, who, like Adam and Eve, walks with God (Gen. 6:9). Despite Noah's righteousness, the earth and the rest of humanity were corrupt and wicked in God's sight, requiring His right judgment. He floods the earth, to wash it of impurity. But God, being rich in mercy, saves Noah and his family through an ark made out of wood. Even in this tragic event, we can see a glimmer of hope that God will one day *save His people through an instrument of wood and nails.*

As the narrative continues, we see humanity doing what they were meant to do—building a kingdom. But instead of cultivating the kingdom of God, humanity establishes a kingdom for themselves.

Genesis 11:4 shows what is in the heart of humanity east of Eden: "Come, let's build ourselves a city and a tower with its top in the sky. Let's make a name for ourselves; otherwise, we will be scattered throughout the earth."

Sinful humanity desires to take the brokenness of this world to heaven. But the perfect King promises to bring heaven to the brokenness of earth.

In His mercy, God thwarts our plans of building our own kingdom, and He scatters humanity throughout the earth. We are no longer citizens of the kingdom, but citizens of Babel.

Remember and Rehearse

Remember through confession and repentance.

One of the most profound aspects of this story is the sinful nature of our hearts after the fall. We don't truly understand ourselves until we remember that, along with Adam and Eve, we have sinned against God. The best way to remember this part of the story is through confession and repentance. When we confess our sin to God and one another, we are acknowledging both our sin and our need for salvation.

The false stories of the world deceive us when they pull us away from the practice of confession and repentance. For example, the false story of perfectionism may tell us that we don't have anything to repent of, just a perfection to strive toward. The biblical story is an invitation to life as we confess and repent.

Rehearse the promises of God.

Rebellion in the kingdom resulted in horrible consequences, but in humanity's darkest moment, God promised a Son who would make things right again. God has invited us to rehearse these promises again and again as we read the story of Scripture with an eye toward the womb of the woman. While there are so many examples of barrenness and brokenness—which I know many of you may have experienced—God will take what was once barren and broken, and He will bring healing and salvation through the Son of a woman. And He will crush the head of the serpent and deliver God's people forever. Forever.

Summary

The story of Genesis 3 is the story of the kingdom lost. Though created to live out God's purposes in the kingdom, God's people rebel against the King, resulting in the loss of God's presence and place.

Discussion Questions

1. How would you tell the story of the kingdom of God lost in the fall?

2. Where do you see the brokenness of the world most clearly (think beyond just sin and depravity)?

3. One of the primary questions of our cultural moment is one of identity: Who are you? But in this story we are asked a different question: Where are you? So, where are you?

- Are you in the presence of God?
- Are you hiding from Him in shame?
- Are you looking for Him?
- Are you safe and secure in His promises?

4. The purpose of God for His people has been disrupted by the corruption of all things through sin. In what ways have you seen this disruption in your own life, work, or relationships?

CHAPTER 6

Covenant with Abraham: The Kingdom Promised

There are some things that are just meant to go together:

- Peanut butter and jelly
- Salt and pepper
- Batman and Robin
- Chips and dip
- Kingdom and covenant

That may sound strange, but stick with me. It's impossible to understand the storyline of Scripture without understanding kingdom and covenant. The Bible is all kingdom and covenant.[10]

Over the course of the next several chapters, we are going to cover a lot of terrain through the storyline of Scripture.

Some portions of Scripture will receive less attention so we can focus on the primary concepts of kingdom and covenant.

The specific covenants we'll look at are:

- The covenant with Abraham (Gen. 12–17)
- The covenant with Moses (Exod. 19–24)
- The covenant with David (2 Sam. 7)
- The new covenant (Jer. 31)

Think of these texts as hot spots or hinges that govern the story of the kingdom.

What Is a Biblical Covenant?

Covenants are not something most of us are familiar with, but in the ancient world covenants were central to life. Powerful kings often entered covenants with other nations, vowing to provide protection and land in exchange for the nation's loyalty. A covenant is like a promise, but it is much more secure than that. They came with clear commitment and consequences if the covenant was broken. These covenants came about through a king's initiative to establish relations with a people. It was not the people who convinced the king to enter a relationship with them, but the powerful king who, through his mercy, enters a relationship with them. Similarly, a biblical covenant is an oath in which the King obligates Himself to a people to establish His kingdom on earth.

Covenants are absolutely central to the storyline of the Bible.

As we trace covenant through the Scripture's storyline, the unity of God's redemptive plan becomes evident. The Bible is not a series of attempts by God to save His people. God is not putting together various plans to see which one may work. God doesn't learn, with each new covenant, another way *not* to save His people. No, the Bible is a story of the singular plan of God to save His people through Christ. Covenants are, therefore, a series of promises that are working together to show God's salvific work for His people.

The Covenant with Abraham

In Genesis 4–11, depravity and death mark the world. Specifically, in chapter 11 we read that humanity attempted to take the kingdom of earth to the kingdom of heaven. In this story with Abraham, God brings the kingdom of heaven to the kingdom of earth.

In Genesis 12, the narrative takes a dramatic turn and focuses its attention on one man, Abraham, and his family. God shows up to Abraham, seemingly out of nowhere, and starts making demands and promises. In Genesis 12:1–3, we read:

> The Lord said to Abraham: "Go from your land, your relatives, and your father's house to the land that I will show you. I will make you into a great nation, I will bless you, I will make your name great, and you will be a blessing. I will bless those who bless you, I will curse anyone who treats you with contempt, and all the peoples on earth will be blessed through you."

This is one of the most pivotal texts in Scripture. What God just promised Abraham is remarkable. He promises to bring the kingdom of God to earth through his family.

The King Promises His Presence

When God says He is going to give Abraham land (we will get to that shortly), He does not just say to him, "Go." He is much more personal than that. He says, "I will show you."

As God reinitiates a relationship with His people, He is doing so in the most intimate terms. God is going to walk with His people again. When God enters into a covenantal relationship with His people, He doesn't just say, "Go"; He says, "Follow Me." The King doesn't just give them a map, He says, "I will show you."

God also tells Abraham, "I will bless you." This language, repeated five times in the story, is set in direct opposition to the language of "curse," also repeated five times in Genesis 3–11. Through Abraham and his family, God is promising to reverse all the effects of the fall. All the curses and consequences will now be turned into blessings.

While prosperity is included in this promise, the ultimate blessing is not material; it is God's presence. We don't just receive things from God, we receive God. His presence is the prize.

I want you to spend a moment contemplating how significant this hope is. Humanity has rebelled against God. The just consequence of that rebellion is shame and exile. But God comes after us. He doesn't wait for us; He pursues us. In this we can see how rich in mercy our King is.

How often in your relationships, when you have been wronged, do you expect the person who has wronged you to come back and ask for forgiveness? What we see in the biblical narrative is that the one we have sinned against initiates the reconciliation of our relationship. He comes to us graciously offering us His presence.

The King Promises to Form a People

God does not only promise His presence, He also obligates Himself to create a new people. In Genesis 11, humanity tries to make a great name for themselves. We, too, often want to build a city that reaches into the heavens.

God laughs at this (Gen. 11:5; Ps. 2), and then scatters and confuses them. They sought greatness and ended up separated. We were never meant to make ourselves great. But God promises to make His people great, not through their impressive feats, but through His family.

God tells Abraham that He will make him into a great nation. God will give him a great name, with no merit earned by Abraham to deserve it.

How often do we desire to distinguish ourselves through accolades, achievement, and our own effort? Are we still, like humanity at Babel, seeking to be known because we build something great? Are we still seeking to build a city that reaches into the heavens?

God is so rich in mercy that we don't have to. The identity of the people of God is not in achieving a great name, but in receiving a great name. The people that God is going to form for Himself represent a new family.

Of course, if you're just reading along, this sounds great. But there's a big problem. Abraham and his wife Sarah are quite old. Not like mid-forties, might-be-a-little-late-to-start-having-kids old—but *really* old. How are they going to be a great nation with a great name if they don't even have a family?

This becomes a struggle for both of them as they wrestle with the promises of God. They cannot see a way forward. Despite the fact that they want to trust God, they begin trusting in their own experience. In some sense, Abraham and Sarah begin to doubt the promises of God because they are trusting their false story.

In Genesis 15, we read,

> After these events, the word of the LORD came to Abram in a vision: "Do not be afraid, Abram. I am your shield; your reward will be very great." But Abram said, "Lord GOD, what can you give me, since I am childless and the heir of my house is Eliezer of Damascus?" Abram continued, "Look, you have given me no offspring, so a slave born in my house will be my heir." (vv. 1–3)

Abraham knows that he can't have a great name and receive a great nation if he doesn't have a child, but how? He begins to wonder who his heir will be, and if God's promises are trustworthy.

God graciously comes to him and says, "This one will not be your heir; instead, one who comes from your own body will be your heir" (v. 4). God's promises will not come any other way but through the womb of the woman.

This is a reminder of both the consequences of our sin and the covenants of salvation (Gen. 3:15–16). Abraham and Sarah are now looking to a barren womb for the promised son who will bring the kingdom.

Not only does God promise them an heir that will come from their own bodies, but it gets better. He promises that their family will outnumber the stars in heaven. Genesis 15:5 says, "He took him outside and said, 'Look at the sky and count the stars, if you are able to count them.' Then He said to him, 'Your offspring will be that numerous.'" Abraham and Sarah go from being childless to being told by God that they will have the largest family on earth. Innumerable and uncountable.

Have you ever struggled to believe the promises of God? So did Abraham and Sarah. They believed that Sarah would never bear a child with Abraham, so they attempted to bring about God's promised through their own means. They attempted to bring about God's promised son by Abraham taking their Egyptian slave Hagar as his wife (Gen. 16:1–5). In their struggle to believe in the promises of God, they took the promises of God into their own hands. When God's people try to sinfully take control of God's promises the result is devastating.

But God remains gracious. He comforts Hagar and He is merciful to Abraham and Sarah.

Even when Abraham doubts the covenantal promises of God, our King promises that His covenant is more gracious and generous than we can ever imagine.

But how does Abraham respond to the promises of God? "Abram believed the LORD, and he credited it to him as righteousness" (Gen. 15:6). Don't miss this. How are God's people made right with God? Faith.

For the rest of the story of Scripture, what distinguishes the people of God is not age, race, ethnicity, socioeconomic status, intellectual ability, gender, or geography. What distinguishes the people of God is faith. God's people trust in the covenants of God.

God's people are reestablished not because of anything they've done, but because of who God is. We receive His promises by grace through faith. We are credited with righteousness through faith alone.

The King Promises a Place

People were made to inhabit a place. At the time that God comes to him, Abraham lives in Ur. Ur is his home. It's familiar. It's what he knows. When God calls Abraham, He tells him to leave his country, his people, and his father's house in order to go to a new place. This is a radical call. His home is Ur, and God calls him to leave all he knows and loves for God's promise of a better home.

Despite the fact that this is a radical call, it is also a gracious call. The promise of a new land is a kind of invitation back to Eden. When Abraham's family is established in the land of Canaan, it is a reminder of God placing the first man in the garden of Eden (Gen. 2:7).

The King is not indiscriminately giving Abraham a new plot of land. Rather, this text is a picture of Abraham re-inheriting the kingdom. Adam was banished, but Abraham is being invited back in. Adam was placed in the kingdom and expelled from it; Abraham was outside the kingdom and is now being brought in.

The King Promises Kingdom Purposes

Embedded in the call of Abraham is not simply that Abraham would be blessed, but that the nations would be blessed through Abraham. The calling of God's people is not meant only for them; they are called to bless the nations.

There is a missionary call to Abraham's family. God does not call Abraham so that the blessings of the kingdom could stop with him. Rather, God calls Abraham and his family to bless all the families of the earth: to be fruitful, multiply, and fill the earth with the image of God. By doing this, they will invite all people to be participants in God reestablishing His kingdom on earth.

In Genesis 12–17, we see a reflection of Genesis 1–2. Adam was planted in a kingdom, but lost it through his rebellion.

The King Who Initiates and Fulfills Covenant

But how do we know this covenant is real? That is exactly the question that Abraham asks God in Genesis 15. He says, "Lord GOD, how can I know that I will possess it?" (v. 8). This is a reasonable question—especially in light of Abraham and Sarah's old age.

Maybe you've felt this way before. Can you trust the promises of God?

In the ancient world, every covenant was accompanied by some kind of ceremony. These ceremonies were meant to bind the two parties together. A covenant was an oath—an oath often entered by blood.

In response to Abraham's question, God says, "Bring me a three-year-old cow, a three-year-old female goat, a three-year-old ram, a turtledove, and a young pigeon" (v. 9).

What in the world? Why would God ask Abraham to bring Him these creatures?

What unfolds in the narrative is nothing short of shocking.

> So he brought all these to him, cut them in
> half, and laid the pieces opposite each other,

> but he did not cut the birds in half. Birds of prey came down on the carcasses, but Abram drove them away. As the sun was setting, a deep sleep came over Abram, and suddenly great terror and darkness descended on him. (vv. 10–12)

This is a terrifying scene. Animals cut in half, laid out opposite one another, forming an aisle. There's blood everywhere. Terror and darkness descend upon Abraham and he falls into a deep sleep.

Asleep?! How could Abraham fall asleep?!

Confusing as it may be, Abraham falling asleep tells us something very important: he has nothing to contribute to the covenant. Only God does. Here's what happened next:

> When the sun had set and it was dark, a smoking fire pot and a flaming torch appeared and passed between the divided animals. On that day the LORD made a covenant with Abram, saying, "I give this land to your offspring." (vv. 17–18)

There are many things about this ceremony that would be familiar to an ancient audience: animals, blood, and two covenant partners. Normally the two covenant partners would walk down the bloody aisle together, signifying that both partners in the covenant will become like these animals if they do not uphold their part of the covenant.

What is most shocking about this covenant is that though there are two partners, they don't walk down the aisle together. The King walks down the aisle by Himself. Abraham contributes nothing. The King walks between the animals who have been cut in half, appearing in smoke and fire, the same symbols we see in Exodus to show the presence of God (Exod. 3:2; 13:21; 19:18).

Amazingly, God is promising He will uphold both His and Abraham's portion of the covenant. The King is also showing Abraham that the King Himself will suffer the consequences if Abraham is unfaithful to the covenant. The King will be a substitute for Abraham if He disobeys the covenant agreement.

True to His word, God provides a son for Abraham and Sarah whose name is Isaac. This is the promised son they have been waiting for. After his birth, God tests Abraham by telling him to offer Isaac as a sacrifice. They set out for Mount Moriah with wood laid on Isaac's back. While preparing the sacrifice, Isaac asks his father, "Where is the lamb for the burnt offering?" Abraham answers simply, "God will provide."

As Abraham is preparing the altar and the sacrifice, an angel of the Lord stops him from sacrificing his son at the last second and God provides a substitute—a sacrificial lamb.

Abraham names the place of the sacrifice, "The Lord Will Provide."

This foreshadows a future event of another Son of Abraham climbing to the top of a mountain with wood on His back. Instead of wood for an altar, it's a wooden cross. And instead of looking for a substitutionary lamb, this Son is the substitutionary lamb; He will wear a crown of thorns and offer a sacrifice that blesses the nations.

The rest of Genesis outlines the stories of Isaac and his sons, Esau and Jacob. Jacob has twelve sons from which the twelve tribes of Israel emerge. One of those sons is sold into slavery in Egypt by his brothers. Due to a great famine in the land, the entire family ends up in Egypt with Joseph, the brother who was sold into slavery, extending forgiveness to his brothers. Even in Egypt, God continues to provide for this family.

But in the midst of God's provision, the question still remains: will God establish His kingdom?

Will God provide the Son who crushes the head of the serpent?

Will God provide the Son of Abraham who offers a substitutionary sacrifice to bless the nations?

Will God restore His kingdom to earth?

Remember and Rehearse

Remember God's faithfulness. He upholds both sides of the covenant.

At the heart of God's covenant with Abraham is His promise to save His people. Looking back at God's promise is a reminder of God's kingdom purpose to save His people through the substitutionary sacrifice of the Son of Abraham.

But the only way Abraham is able to participate in God's covenantal blessings is by grace through faith. The people of God do not have assurance because of what we have promised God, but because of what He has promised us. We contribute nothing to our salvation, but are entirely dependent on the substitutionary sacrifice of a King, the Promised One.

This story invites us to remember that the only way to be in a right relationship with God is through faith. Abraham's life is often a mess, yet he is credited with righteousness because he trusted in the promises of God.

Perhaps your life looks a little bit like Abraham's. Maybe your false story has sent your world into a spiral. Rather than doubling down on your false story hoping that it will provide salvation, you can remember the story of Abraham and believe that relationship with God can be entered into by grace through faith.

Rehearse walking in faith by carrying the good news of Jesus to the nations.

In this story we learn that Abraham's salvation was never meant to terminate on him. We are saved not unto ourselves but unto God and into His purposes. When we take the good news of the gospel to the nations, we rehearse and participate in our missional calling. God's people have been called to be a missionary people (Matt. 28:18–20). When we share the good news with our neighbors and the nations, by proclaiming the gospel, planting churches, and sending missionaries, we are rehearsing the good news that one day people from every nation will praise Jesus as King.

Summary

God graciously makes covenants with His people to establish His kingdom. The covenant with Abraham inaugurates God's ongoing mission to reestablish His kingdom.

Discussion Questions

1. How would you tell the story of the reestablishment of the kingdom of God through God's covenant with Abraham?

2. Read Genesis 12:1–3. What promise does God make to Abraham? How must Abraham trust God to see this promise fulfilled?

3. Read Genesis 15:6. Why was Abraham credited with righteousness? What moments of both faith and doubt occurred in Abraham's life?

4. Read Genesis 15:17–21. What is the significance of God moving between the divided animals in the covenant ceremony?

CHAPTER 7

Covenant with Moses: The Kingdom Kept

God makes promises to Abraham, but does He keep them?

At the conclusion of Genesis, and the beginning of Exodus, God's people are in Egypt, not the place God promised Abraham, Isaac, and Jacob. God sustained His people through a long drought and food shortage by raising up Joseph to a role of leadership in Egypt through a number of unlikely events, and the people of God flourished in Egypt for a time. But a new pharaoh who does not know Joseph and his family takes charge, and he oppresses God's people, making them long for the kingdom of God even more.

God's people cry out to Him for deliverance. They don't simply cry out because of their challenging circumstances.

They also cry out for God to fulfill His covenant. Whenever God's people cry out for the King and the kingdom, God hears. God sees. God knows (Exod. 2:23–25).

In response to Israel's prayers, God raises up a man to deliver His people out of Egypt. In a stunning account, God reveals Himself to Moses in a burning bush. He says,

> "I AM WHO I AM. This is what you are to say to the Israelites: I AM has sent me to you." God also said to Moses, "Say this to the Israelites: The Lord, the God of your ancestors, the God of Abraham, the God of Isaac, and the God of Jacob, has sent me to you. This is my name forever; this is how I am to be remembered in every generation." (Exod. 3:14–15)

In this account, the personal name of God—"I AM," translated "the Lord"—is revealed to Moses. For the first time in Scripture, God reveals His personal name to His people. And in His personal name, we are reminded of both God's transcendence and immanence.

God is the transcendent: "I AM." He is self-existent.

Yet, God is immanent: He comes to His people in a bush.

The "I AM" is also "with us." The transcendent God of the world is knowable. God speaks from heaven, but meets us in the world.

In this exchange, God instructs Moses to assemble the elders of Israel and remind them of the covenant. He says, "I have promised you that I will bring you up from the misery of Egypt to the land of the Canaanites, Hethites, Amorites, Perizzites, Hivites, and Jebusites—a land flowing with milk and honey" (Exod. 3:17).

God is going to take His people back home. To people who have been living in a foreign land as slaves, this is amazing news. God always keeps His covenant (Exod. 6:2–5, 8). But how are God's people going to be brought home?

Moses confronts Pharaoh and, through a series of plagues, the Lord demonstrates His superiority over the so-called gods of Egypt. It is as if God is confronting not just the false gods, but the false stories of Egypt. In the final plague, God instructs the Israelites to sacrifice an unblemished sheep or goat and to wipe the blood around the entryway of their homes because the Lord has come to execute judgment (Exod. 12:1–13). The judgment is the death of every firstborn who is not covered by the blood of a lamb. Even in Exodus, just like in the story of Abraham and Isaac, salvation comes through the sacrificial blood of the lamb, through substitution. That night, every firstborn not covered by the blood of the lamb was killed, but God sees the blood and graciously passes over the firstborn of Israel. As a cry broke out in Egypt, mourning their losses, Pharaoh summoned Moses and Aaron and told them to gather Israel and leave (vv. 29–42).

The title of the book Exodus—which means "the way out"—reminds us that God delivers His people from the kingdom of darkness. The Passover event and subsequent deliverance from Egypt is one of the most dramatic events in Scripture, and one of the most memorable in all of human history. God powerfully delivered His people from their enemies.

After Pharaoh lets Israel go, he makes one last desperate attempt to keep them in Egypt. He sends his armies to capture Israel and bring them back. Israel, stuck between the Red Sea in front and the armies of Pharaoh behind, immediately starts to doubt. But in His grace, God provides a way where there is no way, leading them through the sea on dry ground and swallowing up Pharaoh's armies in the waves as they pursue. God is a mighty warrior who is going to deliver His people into the land He promised them.

The Covenant with Moses

After the Exodus event, God meets His people in the wilderness to offer them another covenant. This covenant found in Exodus 19–24 is once again all about the kingdom of God. The covenant with Moses is characterized by:

- The Holy Presence
- The Holy People
- The Holy Place
- The Holy Purpose

The Holy Presence

One of the most distinctive features of the Exodus narrative is that God is with His people, even in the wilderness. Languishing in exile, God's people cry out to Him. God sees, hears, and delivers them.

God is personally present with His people in Egypt and in the wilderness:

- He meets Moses in the bush (Exod. 3:14).
- He leads them out of Egypt by cloud and by a pillar of fire, physical manifestations of His presence (13:21–22).
- He fights for them at the Red Sea (14:14).
- He rains down bread from heaven for them (16:4).
- He provides water for them from a rock (17:1–7).
- He descends to speak with them in a dense cloud at Mt. Sinai so that the people can hear His voice (19:9).

When we think about the presence of God in Exodus, perhaps the first thing that comes to mind is the presence of God in the tabernacle, but before God takes up temporary residence with His people in the tent, He is with His people in the wilderness and on a mountain.

In the wilderness, God's people came to Sinai. We read,

> Moses went up the mountain to God, and the LORD called to him from the mountain: "This is what you must say to the house of Jacob and explain to the Israelites: 'You have seen what I did to the Egyptians and how I carried you on eagles' wings and brought you to myself. Now if you will carefully listen to me and keep my covenant, you will be my own possession out of all the peoples, although the whole earth is mine, and you will be my kingdom of priests and my holy nation.'" (19:3–6)

God speaks with Moses in a dense cloud, and He tells Moses to consecrate the people. He also instructs Moses to set boundaries around the mountain, because this mountain belongs to the Lord and the Lord is holy (19:9–13).

Sometimes we think of the presence of God as only comforting, but in the story of the Exodus, we see that the holy presence of God is also a fearful thing. God is completely set apart. He is perfectly morally pure. There is nothing else like Him.

A Holy People

Despite the fact that God's people have been living in Egypt for more than four hundred years, God has not left them. He is intent on delivering and forming His people. Specifically, in this narrative we see that the King seeks to form a people who were once slaves into saints.

Living somewhere for four hundred years would rub off on you. Israel undoubtedly had been discipled, shaped, and formed by Egyptian culture. They surely began to even indulge some of the false stories of Egyptian culture. In delivering His people from slavery, God also intends to shape them. His people are not to live like the nations. They are to be holy and set apart.

The storyline of Scripture is not just that God delivers, but that He also sanctifies. He forgives and He forms. God saves sinners. And God sanctifies sinners into saints.

God's people don't belong to themselves. We belong to God. Not only do we belong to God, but we are a kingdom of priests, a holy nation. God's people cannot be like the nations. We are set apart, peculiar, wholly different.

But what do priests do?

Priests function as mediators—representatives. Just as God's people are meant to be image-bearers representing Him to creation, we are now also priests, representing the ways of God to the nations. We are to be holy because God is holy, so to represent Him rightly would be to reflect this holiness in complete devotion to Him.

The Mosaic covenant means that God's people will be in right relationship with God and right relationship with the world. As a nation of priests, they will be the mediators of God's blessings to the world and will be used by God to bring the rest of the world into relationship with Him, echoing the covenant God made with Abraham and his family.

When the nations see Israel, they should see a nation that lives with God. God's people live in a fundamentally different way than the other nations because God dwells with them. The presence of God changes every aspect of our lives. The greatest blessing that God's people can give to the nations is our lives lived before the presence of a holy God. In this way, we reflect the Abrahamic and Mosaic covenants to bless the nations.

The Holy Place

Just like Abraham left the land of Ur for the land of promise, so too Abraham's family leaves the land of Egypt to re-inherit the land of promise, Canaan. But before God's people inherit Canaan, God gives them a temporary place: the tabernacle.

A significant portion of Exodus is God giving instructions about His residence, and they are very particular. It would be easy to glaze over this divine blueprint, like a boring set of unnecessary instructions that don't really apply to us. But this section is uniquely important for understanding the King and His kingdom. We cannot afford to overlook these details because they serve as a reminder to God's people of His desire to be present with them in the land He has graciously given them. God tells us the goal of His home. He says, "I will dwell among the Israelites and be their God. And they will know that I am the LORD their God, who brought them out of the land of Egypt, so that I might dwell among them. I am the LORD their God" (Exod. 29:45–46).

God is coming back to live with His people. They belong to Him because He is their Lord and God. The tabernacle as God's holy place demonstrates four things: 1) the holiness of God, 2) a royal residence, 3) remembrance of Eden, and 4) anticipation of the coming kingdom.

The holy place is a reminder of the holiness of God and the sinfulness of His people. God is holy and we are sinners. It is impossible for sinners to casually enter into the presence of God, and the tabernacle communicates this in several ways. Its design includes successive boundaries, each indicating that anyone entering was getting closer to the holiness of God. In order to enter into His presence, the priests would wear sacred garments and consecrate themselves before offering sacrifices as they entered into the presence of God.

The tabernacle reminds God's people they are entering into a royal residence because God is King. The ornate nature of the furnishings implies the royalty of the person dwelling there, and it's clear you're not just entering the living room of a friend, but the throne room of a king.

The tabernacle is also meant to remind God's people of humanity's origin—Eden. The cherubim that guard the presence of God at the mercy seat, the entrance into the tabernacle from the east, the lampstand resembling the tree of life, and all of the ornate garden decorations in the tabernacle served to remind God's people that they were entering into the presence of God and a kind of Eden.

But it does not just point God's people back to Eden, it also points them forward to a future kingdom God has promised. As we will see in the storyline of Scripture, there is a genuine hope from the people of God that His presence with them won't be temporary and in the wilderness, but permanent and in the land. The temporary tabernacle anticipates a future day when all of God's creation will be His dwelling place (Rev. 21–22).

A Holy Purpose

Arising from the first three points is a clear purpose for God's people. God's people are not just inheriting the kingdom, but the ethics of the King. So God gives them His law in order to teach them about Himself, to restrain moral evil in the world, and to reveal a life that is pleasing to God.

Having spent more than 400 years in Egypt, God's people are in need of reformation, reshaping, and refinement. As Jen Wilkin notes, "They are not just leaving behind the land of Egypt, but also the ways of Egypt."[11]

God graciously gives His people the law in order to give regulations and stipulations for their lives and worship. It is through their obedience and observance to the law that Israel will be a blessing to the nations. The summation of the law is found in the Ten Commandments in Exodus 20:

1. "Do not have other gods besides me" (v. 3).
2. "Do not make an idol for yourself, whether in the shape of anything in the heavens above or on the earth below or in the waters under the earth" (v. 4).
3. "Do not misuse the name of the Lord your God, because the Lord will not leave anyone unpunished who misuses his name" (v. 7).
4. "Remember the Sabbath day, to keep it holy: You are to labor six days and do all your work, but the seventh day

is a Sabbath to the LORD your God" (vv. 8–10).

5. "Honor your father and your mother so that you may have a long life in the land that the LORD your God is giving you" (v. 12).
6. "Do not murder" (v. 13).
7. "Do not commit adultery" (v. 14).
8. "Do not steal" (v. 15).
9. "Do not give false testimony against your neighbor" (v. 16).
10. "Do not covet your neighbor's house. Do not covet your neighbor's wife, his male or female servant, his ox or donkey, or anything that belongs to your neighbor" (v. 17).

Israel's obedience to the law will set them apart as God's people. The law itself is not meant to earn God's favor, because they cannot earn something they already have in full. Before God gives them these commandments, He reminds them who it is they serve, and who it is giving the laws. He is the One who brought them out of Egypt (Exod. 20:1–2). He remembered His covenant and delivered them.

Now He is giving them their calling, their purpose: to be holy. The law is not about earning God's favor; it is about living in light of it.

The Covenant Ceremony

Remember the covenant ceremony with Abraham? Another one takes place in Exodus. In Exodus 24 the covenant is made when God's people agree to do all the Lord commands them (v. 7). Again, it includes a lot of blood and gore. Get ready.

After the people commit themselves to Yahweh and His covenant, Moses makes an animal sacrifice. God tells him to take blood from the animals and splatter it on the people, saying, "This is the blood of the covenant that the LORD has made with you concerning all these words" (Exod. 24:8). God enters into a relationship with His people through the shedding of blood.

Similar to the covenant made with Abraham, the shedding of blood serves as a reminder of the grave nature of a covenantal commitment. Covenantal participants are saying their blood will be shed if they fail to keep the covenant.

After the people are sprinkled with blood, Moses and several elders ascend the mountain. When they ascend the mountain, they see God and have a meal with Him.

Don't miss this moment. The shedding of blood, a conversation with God, and a meal. God is promising, over a meal and through the shedding of blood, to be in fellowship with His people. Sound familiar?

Exodus serves as a kind of birth narrative for the people of God. They've been saved through the waters of the Red Sea, their enemies have been destroyed, and they are born anew as they are delivered from slavery in Egypt in order that they might dwell with God in the land. They have been delivered, and now they are being raised.

Exodus concludes with great news. The King and the kingdom are coming. In the Mosaic covenant we see that God is going to reign and rule with His people once again:

- The King is **present** with His people (Exod. 40:34).
- The King saves and delivers and forms a **people** for Himself. They are people who have been saved and are being sanctified.
- The King has established His **place** among His people, even in the wilderness.
- God graciously gives them His law in order for them to live out their **purpose** of blessing the nations.

The first five books of the Bible continue to tell the story of God's people in the wilderness. God's people journey toward the land promised to Abraham, Isaac, and Jacob. They are being sanctified and shaped so that they may be a people who eventually inherit the King and His kingdom.

Remember and Rehearse

Remember God's people are not to trust in their circumstances, but in the covenants and character of God.

The story of Exodus reminds us that when God's people are living in Egypt, wandering in the wilderness, or living in rebellion, when they cry out to Him, He sees and He hears. God always sees and hears His people.

Regardless of your current situation and circumstance, you can cry out to God. His covenants and His character are trustworthy. God desires to show you that He sees you. He is the covenant-keeping God. And when we call out to Him from our own exile, He always hears and answers.

Remember God saves.

We know that when we cry out to Him, He sees and hears, but He also acts. He acts by sending a deliverer—a Lamb as a perfect substitute—to liberate God's people. But salvation for God's people is more than forgiveness. Salvation includes formation. The blood of the Lamb on the posts of the door would be a sign for what was to come, and the Passover meal would be a rehearsal for a better covenant meal that would be shared by God's people until He returned.

Rehearse the good news that salvation includes formation.

God has not just saved His people, but He also delights in sanctifying His people. He has given us His law in order to show us what He is like, who He is forming us to be, and our need for a Savior. Salvation does not lead us to licentiousness, living however we want. Nor does salvation lead us to legalism, living as if we can merit God's favor. When God gives His law to His people, He does so, so that He might shape and form us into His family.

Rehearse by celebrating the presence of God.

We remember the good news that the same God who dwelt among His people in the tabernacle now dwells in His people by the Spirit. You were made for the presence of God. Rehearse this good news by giving specific attention to the presence of God in your life. We no longer have to go to the tabernacle in order to enjoy the presence of God. Instead, the family of God is now the tabernacling presence of God in the world.

Summary

God delivers His people from the kingdom of darkness into the kingdom of God. At Sinai the covenant-making King is also the covenant-keeping King as He sanctifies a nation of slaves into a kingdom of priests and sons and daughters.

Discussion Questions

1. How would you tell the story of the reestablishment of the kingdom of God through the Exodus and the Mosaic covenant?

2. What is the significance of the tabernacle and the kingdom of God?

3. What does this part of the unfolding kingdom story reveal about God's character? What does it reveal about human nature?

4. How would you describe the holiness of God?

5. How is salvation both forgiveness and formation? How is it both justification (declared right) and sanctification (to be made holy)?

CHAPTER 8

Covenant with David: The Kingdom Expected

After the Mosaic covenant, God's people wander in the wilderness, but eventually are led into the Promised Land. In a very real sense, it feels like the story is reaching a climax. God's people are re-inheriting the land given to Abraham's family. Israel being back in the land is meant to be a foretaste of what God intends for the entire world.

But not everything goes according to plan. God told His people that they needed to expel the Canaanites from the land as they entered. The Canaanites were wicked people who worshipped wicked gods through awful practices of child sacrifice, among other things. God knew that if they were allowed to stay in the land, they would be a snare to the

Israelites. Sure enough, God's people do not obey and are led into idolatry and false worship.

This led to a cycle of sin, defeat, prayer, and deliverance that repeats over and over again in the book of Judges. The people would fall into idolatry, worshipping the Canaanite gods and practicing injustice. God would give them over to their enemies. They would cry out for help, and then God would raise up a judge to deliver His people and call them back to worship God. This cycle—or better said, this spiral downward—results in a sour note at the end of the book of Judges: "there was no king in Israel; everyone did whatever seemed right to him" (Judges 21:25).

Next, the people try a monarchy, asking God for a king like "the other nations" instead of submitting to Yahweh as king (1 Sam. 8:5). They appoint Saul to be their king, but it ends in disaster. Both the failed judges and the failure of Saul's kingdom serve as a reminder that God's people don't owe their survival to a political savior. They are entirely dependent upon the faithfulness of God as their covenantal partner.

But God, being rich in mercy, eventually anoints a different kind of king: King David.

David is the youngest son of a man named Jesse and part of the tribe of Judah, just a shepherd boy and musician at the time he was chosen (1 Sam. 16) as Saul's successor. Before ascending the throne, he courageously kills Goliath and even avoids being murdered by Saul, but what is most notable is his first act as king: bringing the ark, the presence of God, back to Jerusalem. The kingdom is at hand. It is in their midst. The God of heaven is ruling on earth. The good news of the kingdom has been realized. God has been faithful to His covenant.

- For the first time in centuries, God is **present** with His people in the tabernacle established in Jerusalem.
- After governmental failures, God's **people** are being ruled by the king anointed by God.
- After enduring life in Egypt, the Exodus, and wilderness wanderings, God's people are dwelling in the **place** promised to Abraham's family.
- The king delights in the law and desires for God's people to live out the **purposes** God has given them (2 Sam. 7).

As a good reader of the Bible, we should be asking this question. Is this the end of the story? Will the kingdom be established forever right now?

The Covenant with David

This promise of a forever kingdom is given to David in what we call the Davidic covenant. David is ready to establish this kingdom on earth forever, as the text says,

> When the king had settled into his palace and the LORD had given him rest on every side from all his enemies, the king said to the prophet Nathan, "Look, I am living in a cedar house while the ark of God sits inside tent curtains." So Nathan told the king, "Go and do all that is on your mind, for the LORD is with you." (2 Sam. 7:1–3)

David realizes he lives in a cedar house and God is living in a tent! The kingdom is near, but David wants to make it permanent by building a temple—a house—for God's presence, establishing a kingdom with no end. But that night, God comes to the prophet Nathan and offers a different plan. Instead of David building a permanent residence for God, the Lord reverses roles, and says He is going to build a house for David (v. 11). This is a bit of a surprise, because David is already living in a beautiful cedar house, but God is promising to build a different kind of house. This house is more of family house—or a dynasty. This house is characterized by:

- God's eternal presence
- God's eternal people
- God's eternal place
- God's eternal purpose

An Eternal Presence

David understands that at the heart of the storyline of Scripture is the presence of God with His people. Before David ascends to the throne, the ark of God—the place where the glory of the Lord dwells—is captured by the Philistines. God's people are living rebelliously, neglecting the presence of God, and even using His presence as some kind of spiritual rabbit's foot or lucky charm. In their attempt to use God's presence as a tool for their plans, God's presence is exiled from them. To display this in striking fashion, there is even a guy named Ichabod, meaning, "the glory of the Lord has departed."

Yet, in almost comical circumstances, the presence of God among the Philistines wreaks havoc, causing destruction and disease. They eventually recognize what's going on and willingly return the presence to Israel (1 Sam. 5–6).

When David begins his reign, he has the ark moved from Baale-judah to its rightful place in Jerusalem, leaping and dancing before the Lord (2 Sam. 6:16) as it makes its way home. It's not an exaggeration to say that few men have ever desired the presence of God more than David. He writes:

> "In your presence is abundant joy; at your right hand are eternal pleasures." (Ps. 16:11)
>
> "Only goodness and faithful love will pursue me all the days of my life, and I will dwell in the house of the LORD as long as I live." (Ps. 23:6)
>
> "LORD, I love the house where you dwell, the place where your glory resides." (Ps. 26:8)

David is a man preoccupied with the presence of God, preoccupied with building a house for God so that He might live with His people forever. But then, God says to David,

> "Are you to build me a house to dwell in? From the time I brought the Israelites out of Egypt until today I have not dwelt in a house; instead, I have been moving around with a tent as my dwelling. In all my journeys with all the Israelites, have I ever spoken a word to one of the tribal leaders of Israel, whom I commanded to shepherd my people Israel, asking: Why haven't you built me a house of cedar?" (2 Sam. 7:5–7)

It's as if God is saying, "I don't need a house. My dwelling place is with My people." God is reminding David, *I have been with My people, and I am not going anywhere.* While a temple would be built for God, it would not be built by David. Due to his failings, he did not get to see this temple in his lifetime. Instead, his son Solomon would build it (1 Kings 8). But at the heart of the Davidic covenant is not a message of construction, but a message of God's presence eternally with His people.

Do you desire to be in the presence of the Lord the way David did? Do you believe that a moment with Him is better than a hundred years with anybody else?

An Eternal People

From the beginning of Scripture, God has been shaping a people for Himself. We can see an echo of the Abrahamic covenant in God's promise to David when He says, "I will make a great name for you like that of the greatest on the earth" (2 Sam. 7:9).

God covenants with David by promising, "When your time comes and you rest with your ancestors, I will raise up after you your descendant, who will come from your body, and I will establish his kingdom. He is the one who will build a house for my name, and I will establish the throne of his kingdom forever" (2 Sam. 7:12–13).

Remember, at the heart of David's desire is to build a permanent house for the presence of God, but God responds by saying He will build a house for David. David wants to build a grand sanctuary that honors the presence of God. But God denies His request by telling David He is going to build a house for Him.

There is a strange play on words going on here. When David says he wants to build a house, he means a *temple*. When God says He wants to build a house for David, He means a *people*. One day the family of God will also house the presence of God. Here's another way to say it: *David wants to build God a home, but God wants to give David a family.*

An Eternal Place

In the Davidic covenant, God continues to remind His people that He is going to give them a place to dwell. After centuries of exile, wandering, and attempting to establish their place in the land, God continues to graciously offer His people a home. The Lord says,

> I will designate a place for my people Israel and plant them, so that they may live there and not be disturbed again. Evildoers will not continue to oppress them as they have done ever since the day I ordered judges to

> be over my people Israel. I will give you rest from all your enemies. (2 Sam. 7:10–11)

Do you hear the Edenic-like language in this promise?

> I will designate a *place.*
>
> I will *plant* them.
>
> There will be no more *disruption.*
>
> There will be no more *oppression.*
>
> There will be *rest.*

Since the fall, part of the consequences for the people of God has been displacement, but God is promising to plant them again. This garden imagery reminds us of the home we lost, Eden, and the promise of a home waiting for us.

But this place is not just a garden, it is also a kingdom. God says to David that his son "will build a house for my name, and I will establish the throne of his kingdom forever" (2 Sam. 7:13). Don't miss this. In this covenant, God is promising to give His people a garden-kingdom, a place of *shalom,* which is the Hebrew word for true peace and harmony. This *shalom* is only possible because God reigns from the throne.

An Eternal Purpose

In the Davidic covenant, God promises to establish His eternal purposes through a new King. One day God's people will not follow wicked, unjust, and unrighteous kings, but rather God will raise up an eternal King to the throne. This King will reign and rule for the glory of God. Unlike every other king and kingdom from the past, this King and kingdom, "will be established forever" (2 Sam. 7:16).

One day, the eternal purpose of humanity, which is to reign and rule by giving God glory, will be accomplished through the line of David and His kingdom. This King will give glory to God in all things. He will reign and rule with righteousness and justice.

In the same way that Adam and Eve were meant to image the glory of God to all creation, the kingdom of Christ, through David, will accomplish God's purposes forever, so that all nations will witness the glory of God.

In the Davidic covenant, God is giving His people a covenant that has everything to do with the kingdom.

- God will be **present** with His people forever.
- God will raise up a family of **people** who live for the glory of God.
- God will give His people a **place** that is shaped by the peace of God's kingdom.

- God will accomplish His **purpose** for humanity by raising up a King and a kingdom whose throne will be established forever.

The Temple Built

David's son, Solomon, did build a temple for the Lord. In both a fulfillment of the covenant, and a foreshadowing of the future fulfillment of the new covenant brought by Jesus, God comes to dwell with His people in Solomon's temple. As the temple is complete,

> The priests and the Levites brought the ark of the LORD, the tent of meeting, and the holy utensils that were in the tent. King Solomon and the entire congregation of Israel, who had gathered around him and were with him in front of the ark, were sacrificing sheep, goats, and cattle that could not be counted or numbered, because there were so many. (1 Kings 8:4–5)

God's people are preparing for God to establish His kingdom on earth. After the ark is moved into the Holy of Holies, the priests exit the newly built temple and God comes to dwell with His people. We read, "When the priests came out of the holy place, the cloud filled the LORD's temple, and because of the cloud, the priests were not able to continue ministering, for the glory of the LORD filled the temple" (vv. 10–11).

Is this it? Has God finally established His kingdom on earth forever?

God is **present** with His **people** in the **place** He has given them as they live out His **purpose** for them. Solomon seems to think that the kingdom has been established. He stands before God and His people and prays,

> "LORD God of Israel, there is no God like you in heaven above or on earth below, who keeps the gracious covenant with your servants who walk before you with all their heart. You have kept what you promised to your servant, my father David. You spoke directly to him and you fulfilled your promise by your power as it is today." (vv. 23–24)

Solomon acknowledges that God is the gracious covenant-making and covenant-keeping God. In many ways, it appears that the kingdom of God has come to earth in its fullness. But even this is only pointing forward to a fuller, truer, better Son of David.

Remember and Rehearse

Remember the promise of God's presence.

God came to dwell with His people in the temple that Solomon built, but this was only a shadow of the presence that was to come for His people. The family of God would one day be called the house or the tabernacling presence of God.

For the Christian, this isn't just good news to remember, but also good news to rehearse. In the same way that God filled the temple that Solomon built in 1 Kings 8, He has filled you with His Holy Spirit. Rehearse the good news that God has come to dwell in you.

Rehearse the promise of the coming kingdom.

There comes a day when Jesus will reign and rule over all the earth from the new Jerusalem. As we eagerly await His return, we can pray in the same way that He taught His disciples to pray: "Your kingdom come. Your will be done on earth as it is in heaven" (Matt. 6:10). Disciples of Jesus can pray these words with confidence because we remember that God brought a shadow of His kingdom through Solomon, David's son, but one day He will bring the fullness of His kingdom through the true Son of David, Jesus Christ.

Summary

God will establish His kingdom forever by raising up a King who will reign and rule forever. In the Davidic covenant, the covenant-keeping God promises to reestablish His kingdom on earth.

Discussion Questions

1. How would you tell the story of the reestablishment of the kingdom of God through the Davidic Covenant?

2. How does the Davidic covenant and the promise of an eternal kingdom help you to see through the false promises of the story or stories you are living in?

3. Why is God's promise to build a "house" for David so significant and so shocking?

4. Read 1 Kings 8 and Acts 2. What parallels do you see?

5. The presence of God in His temple is central to the Davidic covenant. How do we live aware of His presence in His people, His temple, today?

CHAPTER 9

Covenant in Exile: The Kingdom in Darkness

In an instant, everything can change. A surprise breakup, job loss, diagnosis, or injury can slam your life's brakes, spinning you into chaos as you try to make sense of which way is forward.

This is the emotional inertia found in moving from the last chapter to this one. In the last chapter, it looked as if the kingdom of God had been established on earth. Presence, people, purpose, place. All of it. Things were going *great.*

Don't you wish the story ended there? God has been faithful to His covenant. He has delivered His people from darkness. He has established them in the land promised to Abraham's family. He is present with His people as they dwell in the land. Not only that, but they have been given peace from their enemies. Solomon's temple has been established and it is glorious. Heaven on earth. The kingdom of God is here.

But it doesn't take long for the rebellion of God's people to obscure this glimpse of the kingdom again. It was the pattern of the people, and the pattern of their kings.

David grievously sinned against the Lord and Bathsheba. Solomon walked in his own rebellion and disobedience forcing God's people into labor, rejecting God's instructions and abandoning godly wisdom. And Rehoboam—Solomon's son and successor—committed to oppressing God's people more than Solomon had, resulting in the division of God's people into two separate kingdoms.

These two kingdoms, the Northern Kingdom of Israel and the Southern Kingdom of Judah, are primarily ruled by wicked and idolatrous kings who forget the Lord and His law. You could say that God's people begin living into their own false stories, just like we do. These kings seek power, comfort, and distraction, everything but the kingdom of God.

But God does not give His people over to their wickedness; even in the midst of humanity's rebellion, He graciously sends prophets to His people to warn them of coming judgment and call them to turn back to faithfulness. The message of the prophets was one of repentance, calling God's people to "Repent, for the kingdom of heaven is at hand." Their message reminded God's people of their covenant with the

Lord and how there would be serious consequences for their disobedience.

Hosea, for example, pictures God's people as an adulterous wife wandering from her husband, the Lord. Prophets like Amos, Elijah, Elisha, Jeremiah, and others contend with God's people to repent from their rebellion and to return to the Lord. Their message is that unless God's people repent, return to the Lord, and obey Him, God will send judgment.

God's people ignore His many warnings and pleadings through the prophets and disaster strikes. They ultimately reject His covenant by refusing to return to covenant faithfulness, so consequences come: God's people are sent back into exile.

Sound familiar?

The exile of God's people is a shadow of humanity's first exile from the garden, as Israel and Judah are cast out of the land, just like Adam and Eve.

In 722 BC, the Northern Kingdom was conquered by the Assyrians. Shortly after, in 605, 597, and 586 BC, the Southern Kingdom was taken into captivity by the Babylonians. Notably, the prophets were quick to tell God's people this exile was not at the hands of their captors, but was orchestrated by God. The kingdom rebels, and its people are cast out of the kingdom by the king.

We can't skip over how important this event was. For God's people, this is not just a historical event. It is a theological, or spiritual, event. God pronounces judgment upon His people. The consequences of their sin is the kingdom lost, *again.*

God removes His **presence**. God exiles His **people**. God's **place**, the temple, has been destroyed and lies in ruins. All because God's people did not live out the **purpose** God gave them.

God's people are once again living east of Eden. Exile always leads to the tower of Babel or to the kingdom of Babylon. Doesn't it seem like we've read this before?

Hope in Exile

In exile, God's people are tempted to ask: How did we get here? Can we trust God's covenants? Is God faithful? Or is God done with us?

Not only did God send prophets to His people before they were sent into exile, warning them of the consequences of their disobedience, God continues to send prophets to His people while they are in exile. Their primary message was one of hope, it was one of the kingdom.

If the prophetic message before exile was, *turn back, or there will be serious consequences,* the message during exile is, *even though you failed to turn back to God, He will not turn away from you.*

The message of the prophets to God's people in exile was all about the kingdom. They reminded God's people that their rebellion led them to judgment, but that judgment is not the end of the story. Despite the faithlessness of the people, God would remain faithful to His covenant. He takes the divine initiative to maintain a relationship with them.

Everything the prophets say is grounded in the biblical covenants. Based upon the covenants, the prophets proclaim to God's people: You have been unfaithful, but the Lord remains faithful. God is going to execute judgment, but He is also going to bring salvation. God is going to discipline you for your sin, but He is also going to save you from your sin. The message of the prophets is both one of judgment and one of deliverance.

Judgment because of the wickedness of God's people.

Deliverance because of the faithfulness of God.

At the heart of their message is the new covenant.[12]

Even when they are living among the Assyrians and the Babylonians and the nations, God comes to His people to remind them that one day exile will end and the kingdom will be established forever through a new and better covenant. In the new covenant, God promises to bring His kingdom forever.

The Promise of Presence in Exile

God promises His people the new covenant while they are in exile through the prophet Jeremiah, who writes, "'Look, the days are coming'—this is the LORD's declaration—'when I will make a new covenant with the house of Israel and with the house of Judah'" (Jer. 31:31). Just this simple declaration is amazing news to people who are living in the consequences of their sin.

God moves toward His covenantal people, even when they've been disobedient. When people hurt or reject us, we tend to move away from them; not so with God—He moves toward His people in love. Sin has real consequences, but God's grace is greater.

God is being merciful. He does not just say that He will be faithful to the covenants given to Abraham, Isaac, and Jacob. He will be. He goes further than that. He actually says He is going to give them a new covenant.

But what is new about it? One thing that is new about the new covenant is the presence of God.

It isn't new *that* God promises He will be present with His people. We already know that. What is new is *where* God promises to be present with His people. Ezekiel reveals this in 11:19: "I will give them integrity of heart and put a new spirit within them; I will remove their heart of stone from their bodies and give them a heart of flesh."

In the new covenant, God does not just promise to be *with* His people. God promises to be *in* His people. In the new covenant the Spirit does not simply dwell in a temple or tabernacle, but inside every member of the new covenant community, the family of God. This points us back to Eden when God first breathed the breath of life into Adam's lungs.

The new covenant also involves a work of the heart. God promises to give His people a new heart—to give them new life, or what we call *regeneration*. God's people are like a valley of dry bones, but one day God will "put breath in you so that you come to life" (Ezek. 37:6). God is going to make dead people come alive and "pour out my Spirit on all humanity," so that "everyone who calls on the name of the LORD will be saved" (Joel 2:28–32).

A shocking element of the new covenant is that God's presence will not just be *available* to God's people, but it will be *in* God's people.

God's People in Exile

The sin of God's people was the cause of their exile, and their greatest need wasn't to return to their cities, but to return to their God so that their sins may be forgiven. And that's exactly what the new covenant promises. At the very heart of the new covenant lies the good news of forgiveness of sin. God's people will no longer be identified as the people who have sinned against the Lord, but they will be the people who have been forgiven by the Lord. God says of His people, "I will forgive their iniquity and never again remember their sin" (Jer. 31:34).

I promise you, this is the best news you've ever heard—especially if you've realized your sin has led you to be separated from God. The greatest need of every single person is to have their sin forgiven by a holy God, so they can be brought back into His presence. In the new covenant we hear two beautiful truths from God:

> First, "I will forgive your sin and iniquity."
>
> Second, "I will never again remember it."

The primary characteristic of God's people isn't sinfulness. The primary character of God's people is we have had our sins forgiven.

With our sins forgiven, we can be God's people again, as God proclaims through the prophet Jeremiah, "I will be their God, and they will be my people" (Jer. 31:33). And we are freed to live with confidence that this will not be taken from us because God proclaims He will remember our sin no more.

Isaiah, reflecting on the new covenant, says, "All who see them will recognize that they are a people the Lord has blessed" (Isa. 61:9). Indeed, as the psalmist says, "How joyful is the one whose transgression is forgiven, whose sin is covered! How joyful is a person whom the Lord does not charge with iniquity" (Ps. 32:1–2).

God's Purpose in Exile

At the heart of the Mosaic covenant was the call for God's people to covenantal obedience to an external law. This was their purpose—to live according to the law of God.

Exile was, in a very real sense, Israel's punishment for their failure to live up to this law. God told them through Moses, before they entered the Promised Land, that if they rejected Him and worshipped other gods and turned their hearts away from Him, they would be expelled from the land. Sure enough, when they failed to live up to the law, they were exiled.

But in exile, through the prophets, God promised to do something different with the law. In the new covenant, He wouldn't write it on stone tablets, but on the human heart (Jer. 31:33). His people in the future would be able to obey the law because, just like His Spirit, the law would now be placed inside of them. Therefore, all of God's people will know the Lord, from the least to the greatest (Jer. 31:34).

The Hope of Place in Exile

While living in exile, God's people longed to return to the place given to Abraham, Isaac, and Jacob. They longed for the land. They longed to rebuild the temple. They longed for the kingdom of God. During Babylonian rule, there was no hope of God's people being allowed to return to the place God had given them.

But in God's providence, Babylonian rule did not last forever. The Persians, in 539 BC, defeated the Babylonians and had a very different policy toward the exiles. The books of Ezra and Nehemiah tell a story of return to the land.

In the Hebrew Scriptures, the books of Ezra and Nehemiah are actually one book and connecting stories. Much like the stories of Abraham leaving Ur and God's people leaving Egypt, the stories of Ezra and Nehemiah signify a new exodus for God's people, a story of God delivering His people into the land He has given them.

Ezra begins with the story of King Cyrus of Persia proclaiming a new decree that the exiles could return and rebuild the temple in Jerusalem. But the rebuilding of a temple was not like the rebuilding of any structure. It was an effort to see God's presence return to the land.

Similarly, Nehemiah returns to the land in order to build a wall of protection around Jerusalem, where God's people—and more importantly—God's presence would dwell. Nehemiah is a man who believes in the covenantal promises of God, believing that the Lord will again dwell with His people in this place.

Once the walls and temple are rebuilt, God's people are eager for the presence of the Lord to return, as it did when Solomon built the temple (1 Kings 8). As the temple was completed, a loud noise rose from God's people, but it wasn't all shouting. Ezra 3:10–13 says:

> When the builders had laid the foundation of the LORD's temple, the priests, dressed in their robes and holding trumpets, and the Levites descended from Asaph, holding cymbals, took their positions to praise the LORD, as King David of Israel had instructed. They sang with praise and thanksgiving to the LORD: "For he is good; his faithful love to Israel endures forever." Then all the people gave a great shout of praise to the LORD because the foundation of the LORD's house had been laid. But many of the older priests, Levites, and family heads, who had seen the first temple, wept loudly when they saw the foundation of this temple, but many others shouted joyfully. The people could not distinguish the sound of the joyful shouting from that of the weeping, because the people were shouting so loudly. And the sound was heard far away.

This is the moment God's people were waiting for. They have returned to the land to rebuild the temple and the wall, signifying that God's people are back in the place that God has given them, living out His purposes in the presence of the Lord in the temple. They are celebrating God's faithful covenantal love!

But then something interesting happens. The older priests, Levites, and family leaders who had seen the first temple begin to weep. Why? They don't weep because of the construction of the temple. They weep because the temple is still lacking God's presence.

Despite the fact that they are back in the land, they are still in exile. They are in God's place but still waiting for God's presence.

Unanswered Questions

As the Old Testament comes to a close, these questions remain:

- Will we experience the presence of God again?
- Will God restore His people?
- Will God give His people a permanent place to dwell?
- Will we live out the purposes God has given us?
- Where is the Son of a woman who will come to crush the head of the serpent?

- Where is the Son of Abraham who will come to offer a sacrifice that blesses the nations?
- Where is the Lamb of God who will take away the sins of the world?
- Where is the Son of David who will come to establish a kingdom without end?
- Will God ever initiate the new covenant with His people?

For 400 years between the Old and New Testaments, God's people are watching and waiting, while these questions remain unanswered. For centuries they live under Persian, Greek, and Roman kingdoms, in various levels of freedom and oppression, comfort and suffering as they wait.

Even in exile, we are reminded that God has placed all of His covenantal promises on one descendant, one Son, one seed.

God has promised to bring His kingdom through the Son of a woman who will crush the head of the serpent (Gen. 3:15).

God has promised to bring His kingdom through the Son of Abraham who will bless the nations through His sacrifice (Gen. 12–22).

God has promised to make His people a kingdom of priests (Exod. 19–24).

God has promised to bring His kingdom through the Son of David, who will build a temple and establish an eternal throne forever (2 Sam. 7).

God has promised to bring His kingdom into our hearts through the Holy Spirit. He will bring the dead to life and will write His law upon our hearts (Jer. 31:31–34).

Remember and Rehearse

Remember God's faithfulness.

False stories are powerful in exile. Exile is disorienting, and it leads us to question the biblical story. Maybe the story of the Babylonians is the true story? Maybe the false stories of romanticism, perfectionism, consumerism, or politicalism are true? Maybe we should hedge our bets and not give everything to the kingdom? Undoubtedly, God's people would have been tempted to put their trust in the false stories of Babylon.

One of the most important things God's people can do when living in exile is remember God's faithfulness. Even when we can't see what He is doing, we remember His faithfulness to the covenant. He has never left or abandoned His people. We can live faithfully in the present when we remind ourselves of God's faithfulness to us in the past.

Even now, what are ways God has been faithful to you in the past? What can you recall and remember? How has He met you in your greatest moments of need?

Rehearse the future events of the kingdom.

While living in exile, God's people are also called to rehearse the future events of the kingdom. In exile, the best news is that God's kingdom is coming. We delight in the good news that our exile will not last forever, but that our King and His kingdom will one day come in their fullness.

There are two ways God's people can rehearse the future events of the kingdom. First, God's people are called to repentance. God's people were still living in exile when Jesus and His disciples preached a message of repentance that God's kingdom was at hand. We rehearse the future events of the coming kingdom when we take our sin and rebellion seriously and repent.

Second, we rehearse the events of the kingdom when we, in faith, wait patiently for the Lord to return. We, along with God's people for two millenia, ask God to bring His kingdom. O Come, O Come Emmanuel.

We rehearse the events of the kingdom through repentance and faith because God's kingdom is at hand.

Summary

Even in exile, when God's people have lost God's presence, lost their place, and lost their purpose, God sends hope, reminding them that one day His kingdom will come in fullness.

Discussion Questions

1. How would you tell the story of God's people and their disobedience leading to exile? How would you incorporate the new covenant?

2. How has your sin led to exile from God in your lifetime? How did God bring you back home?

3. All of our false stories are ultimately stories from exile. These stories are designed to blind us from the true story of the world, convincing us that this is all there ever will be, so we might as well enjoy it and find comfort in it. How does your false story provide a false sense of comfort in exile?

4. What ways can you combat your false story by remembering and rehearsing God's covenants?

5. How can God's family play an important role in combating your false stories?

CHAPTER 10

Christ: The Good News of the King and His Kingdom

"Victory!" This headline described the unconditional surrender of Nazi Germany in World War II.

Headlines capture attention, and good ones make you want to keep reading. The best headlines are those you've wished for, dreamed about, and waited on. Imagine the rejoicing for those who had long lamented the terrible atrocities at the hands of Nazi Germany on the day "Victory" was at the top of their papers.

That's exactly how the New Testament begins. "An account of the genealogy of Jesus Christ, the Son of David, the Son of Abraham" (Matt. 1:1).

It is hard to imagine a better opening line for the New Testament. God is bringing His kingdom through the Son of a woman, the Son of Abraham, the Son of David. This is the moment. This is the good news, the gospel. It's as if He is shouting from the rooftops:

> This is the new beginning, initiated by the birth of Jesus Christ.
>
> Jesus Christ is the Son of a woman who has come to crush the head of the serpent.
>
> Jesus Christ is the Son of David who has come to establish God's kingdom.
>
> Jesus Christ is the Son of Abraham who has come to offer a sacrifice that will bless the nations.

The good news of Jesus is found in the first sentence of the Gospel of Matthew. I am sure you have read Matthew 1:1 before, but perhaps you've never understood what Matthew is trying to say. This is not any genealogy. This is a genealogy to show us that in Christ, God kept all of His promises.

The Old Testament ended with a series of questions related to whether or not God would establish His kingdom, and the first line of the New Testament answers that question with a resounding, "Yes!"

Jesus Christ and the Presence of God

The birth of Jesus is anything but ordinary. It is a story about angels, dreams, a nativity, a miraculous virgin birth, and the Holy Spirit. It is a wild story! But all of these things take place, Matthew tells us, to fulfill Old Testament prophecy:

> Now all this took place to fulfill what was spoken by the Lord through the prophet: See, the virgin will become pregnant and give birth to a son, and they will name him Immanuel, which is translated "God is with us." (Matt. 1:22–23)

The whole story is reaching its climax: God with us. This is the central claim of the Christian faith: God took on flesh to dwell among us, live a perfect life, die a substitutionary death in our place, and defeat death forever in His resurrection.

What an amazing claim! Throughout the story of the Bible, where have we seen God be present with His people? A garden. A bush. A tabernacle. A temple. But now, God has come to us in the flesh in the person of Jesus Christ.

The Gospel of John makes the exact same claim. John begins his Gospel by claiming,

> In the beginning was the Word, and the Word was with God, and the Word was God. He was with God in the beginning. All

> things were created through him, and apart from him not one thing was created that has been created. In him was life, and that life was the light of men. That light shines in the darkness, and yet the darkness did not overcome it. (John 1:1–5)

But he also tells us, "The Word became flesh and dwelt among us. We observed his glory, the glory as the one and only Son from the Father, full of grace and truth" (John 1:14). Don't miss this. John is telling us that the eternal Word of God has taken on flesh to dwell among His people.

The term John uses to communicate that the Word came to dwell among us is the exact same word that the Greek translation of the Old Testament uses for "tabernacle." The eternal Word, the Son of God, has come to "tabernacle" among us. Jesus Christ is the tabernacling presence of God. God dwells with us in Christ. The apostle Paul uses similar language in his letter to the Colossians saying, "For God was pleased to have all his fullness dwell in him" (Col. 1:19). The *fullness* of God came to dwell with us in Christ.

I want you to think about what a significant claim this is. The entire storyline of the Bible going all the way back to Eden has been about the kingdom of God: the kingdom established and the kingdom lost. We wander this world looking for the presence of God, but because of our rebellion and disobedience, much of our experience is brokenness, sin, and exile.

But God is so rich in mercy that He does not just invite us back into His presence. He comes to us. The light of the world has come into the darkness and the darkness cannot overcome it (John 1:5). God has come to be present with His people and to seek and save the lost (Luke 19:10).

In the midst of all of our false stories, one of our deepest inclinations is to make God in our own image. But because of the incarnation, we are invited no longer to make God in our image, but to worship the only true image of God, Jesus Christ. We don't have to guess what God is like; we just have to look at Jesus. And when our ideas about God are inconsistent with the person of Christ, His life is a corrective. God in our own image is no god to be worshipped, but an idol to be killed. The God of the Bible has revealed Himself in Christ. To know Him is to know God, and you cannot know God without knowing Christ. He is Immanuel. He is the exact expression of God's nature and character. He is God with us.

Jesus Christ and the Purpose of God

Jesus came to establish the kingdom of God and to reign as King. At the very heart of Jesus's ministry and purpose is the kingdom of God. The Gospel writers go to great lengths to show how Jesus is the King we have been waiting for.

Not only is His genealogy tied to the Son of Abraham and the Son of David, He is also declared to be the King of the Jews (Matt. 2:2); He is anointed as a King in His baptism; and His teaching ministry consists almost entirely of teaching about the kingdom of God, which can be summed up as: "Repent, because the kingdom of heaven has come near" (Matt. 4:17).

Whether He is talking to Sadducees or Pharisees, tax collectors or Samaritans, enormous crowds or in synagogues, He has essentially one message: the kingdom.

> The kingdom of heaven is like a sower (Matt. 13:18–23).
>
> The kingdom of heaven is like a man who sowed seed in his field (v. 24).
>
> The kingdom of heaven is like a mustard seed (v. 31).
>
> The kingdom of heaven is like leaven (v. 33).
>
> The kingdom of heaven is like hidden treasure buried in a field (v. 44).
>
> The kingdom of heaven is like a merchant in search of fine pearls (v. 45).
>
> The kingdom of heaven is like a net (v. 47).
>
> The kingdom of heaven is like a storeroom of new and old treasures (v. 52).

It is impossible to understand who Jesus is or the purpose He came to accomplish without understanding the kingdom of God. It is absolutely central to who He is and what He came to do.

The disciples knew this. That's why the disciples began following Him. They believed His ministry was an in-breaking of the kingdom on earth. That's why they ask Him questions like, "Who will get to sit at Your right and left hand in the kingdom?" (see Mark 10:37). They are convinced the purpose of Jesus's ministry is to establish the kingdom of God on earth.

But then the Gospels begin to tell a story they (and we) were not expecting—a story of a different kind of King and an upside-down kingdom.

As Jesus travels and teaches His disciples, He asks them who people say He is. They answer, "Some say John the Baptist; others, Elijah; still others, Jeremiah or one of the prophets" (Matt. 16:14). But then Jesus asks a more pointed question. He wants to know who they think *He* is. Simon Peter answers, "You are the Messiah, the Son of the living God" (v. 16). Jesus responds to Peter, saying, "Blessed are you, Simon son of Jonah, because flesh and blood did not reveal this to you, but my Father in heaven" (v. 17).

Peter gets it right. Jesus is the King, the Anointed One. Jesus is the Messiah. Jesus has come for the purpose of establishing the kingdom. But then Jesus reveals to the disciples that His may not be the kingdom they are expecting. He tells them, it is "necessary for him to go to Jerusalem and suffer many things from the elders, chief priests, and scribes, be killed . . ." (v. 21).

What? How could this be possible? Isn't Jesus's ministry an establishment of God's purpose? Isn't He here to bring the kingdom of God? How could He be headed toward death?

Peter rebukes Jesus in verse 22, saying, "Oh no, Lord! This will never happen to you!" (Side note: It is never a good idea to rebuke Jesus.) He responds to Peter and says, "Get behind me, Satan! You are a hindrance to me because you're not thinking about God's concerns but human concerns" (v. 23). In other words, *You still don't understand what kind of a King I am and what kind of a kingdom I am bringing.* Jesus essentially tells Peter that he is living in a false story.

Peter gets the identity of Jesus right, but he misunderstands what Jesus is really all about. It is not enough to know who Jesus is if you don't know why He came. For Peter, the story of the kingdom of God, the story of God's presence, God's people, God's purpose, and God's place can't include a Roman cross. A King should be powerful, ruling however He sees fit. A true king comes to conquer his enemies, not be conquered by them on a cross. How can Jesus be King if He is hanging lifeless on a Roman cross? A dead King serves no purpose.

I think if we are honest, we all are like Peter. How can a dead King accomplish the purposes of the kingdom of God? Kings don't die on crosses. They rule from thrones.

Jesus Christ and the Place of God

When Jesus told Peter, and the rest of the disciples, that He was on His way to the place of the cross, they still did not understand all Jesus meant. Why would Jesus claim to be the King, but also predict His death at the hands of the Romans on a cross?

When Jesus enters Jerusalem, the place of God and God's people, He is given a King's welcome. Matthew tells us He enters on a donkey in order to fulfill what was spoken through the prophet, "See, your King is coming to you, gentle, and mounted on a donkey, and on a colt, the foal of a donkey" (Matt. 21:5; see Zech. 9:9).

The crowd shouts praise to their king, chanting, "Hosanna to the Son of David! Blessed is he who comes in the name of the Lord! Hosanna in the highest heaven!" (Matt. 21:9). Do you see what they are saying about Him? *This is the Son of David! This is the King who has come to save and deliver us! This is the One who has come to establish God's throne forever. The Son of David has finally come back to Jerusalem to establish the kingdom of God forever.*

When Jesus and His disciples gather to celebrate the Passover meal, instituted to celebrate their deliverance from Egypt, Jesus totally reorients this important meal. Instead of telling the story of the Exodus, He begins to talk about Himself. Matthew tells us,

> Jesus took bread, blessed and broke it, gave it to the disciples, and said, "Take and eat it; this is my body." Then he took a cup, and after giving thanks, he gave it to them and said, "Drink from it, all of you. For this is my blood of the covenant, which is poured out for many for the forgiveness of sins. But I tell you, I will not drink from this fruit of the vine from now on until that day when I drink it new with you in my Father's kingdom." (26:26–29)

Instead of talking about the Passover of the past, Jesus is essentially saying He is the sacrificial Lamb. And did you notice the language Jesus uses to describe His death? He uses the language of covenant. Jesus is saying that a new Passover is coming to bring about a new covenant.

Not only does He reorient the elements around Himself, He tells His disciples that His life and death are all about covenant.

God promised to crush the head of the serpent.

God promised to send the Son of Abraham who will offer a sacrifice to bless the nations.

God promised His people would be a kingdom of priests who offer sacrifices for the atonement of sin.

God promised to send the Son of David who will establish an eternal kingdom and reign from an eternal throne.

God promised His Spirit and Law would be written on the hearts of His people.

Essentially, Jesus is telling His disciples to have their mind's eye the entirety of the Old Testament and the covenants. He is saying, *God makes covenants, and I am here to fulfill them. God has promised and I am here to deliver on those promises.*

After this, we get to the final hours of Jesus's life (or so it would seem). These hours are described in such an astonishing way. Not only is the brutality with which they treat Jesus hard to fathom, there is also something else going on in the story. Let's see if you can pick up on it.

Matthew writes, "They stripped him and dressed him in a scarlet robe. They twisted together a crown of thorns, put it on his head, and placed a staff in his right hand. And they knelt down before him and mocked him: 'Hail, king of the Jews!'" (27:28–29).

They placed a sign above His head that read, "THIS IS JESUS, THE KING OF THE JEWS" (v. 37).

Earlier, as Jesus was teaching in the synagogue, He taught that He would destroy and rebuild the temple in three days, and while He was revealing what was to come with His death and resurrection, the leaders did not understand. At the crucifixion, the crowd mocks Him for this claim. They say, "You who would destroy the temple and rebuild it in three days, save yourself! If you are the Son of God, come down from the cross!" (v. 40). When Jesus claimed He could build the temple in three days, He was not just making a miraculous claim; He was making a claim of kingship.

It's as if they are saying, "Some king. He said He'd build the temple, but there He is on the cross."

Luke tells us about the criminals being crucified with Him. One hurls insults at Jesus, but the other criminal says, "Jesus, remember me when you come into your kingdom" (Luke 23:42).

What story are the Gospel writers telling? They are telling the story of the enthronement of a king. Did you notice it?

Jesus is given a royal robe, a crown of thorns, and a king's staff. They mock Him by saying, "Hail, King of the Jews." They mock His claim of being the king who will build a temple. They even place a sign above His head stating He is the King of the Jews.

Yet, the first person to recognize the true kingdom and kingship of Christ is the man being crucified next to Him. Even Peter didn't see this coming.

Jesus is not simply King after the cross; Jesus is the King on the cross. The cross is not simply a Roman executionary device; it is a throne. The crucifixion isn't just an execution; it's a coronation.

The cross is the place, the throne, by which God is establishing His kingdom.

The Son of a woman has come to crush the head of the serpent at Golgotha—the place of the skull (Gen. 3:15; Matt. 27:33).

The Son of Abraham, with the wood laid on His shoulders, has come to offer a sacrifice that will bless the nations (Gen 22:6–14; John 19:17–41).

The Son of David, seated on the throne of the cross, has come to establish God's eternal kingdom (2 Sam. 7:13; Matt. 27:27–44).

The crucifixion of Jesus is an enthronement ceremony. The King of the cosmos has come to reclaim all that was lost in Eden. The Son of a woman, the Son of David, the Son of Abraham is now King.

This is the ultimate reversal. The kings of this world exert their power by putting others on crosses, but the King of heaven rules by putting Himself there. The fruit of the tree in the garden brought death and exile; the fruit of the tree of the cross brings life and invitation into the kingdom. The cross is the place of God by which He establishes His kingdom on earth forever.

Jesus Christ and the People of God

In Jesus Christ, God is with us. He has come to establish the kingdom of God. And the cross is the place where God initiates the invasion of the kingdom into this world. But what does that mean for the people of God?

We are still marked by sin. We are, by nature, rebels. We are in need of forgiveness. We are in need of reconciliation.

Throughout the story of Scripture, we know that the only way for God's people to be made right with God is through atonement. Atonement refers to the reconciliation or restoration of the broken relationship between God and humanity through sacrifice. Sacrifice is the key here. Remember, the consequences of our sin in Genesis 3 are death and separation from God. To overlook this necessary consequence would make God unjust, and even a liar. The penalty for sin must be paid and the wages of sin is death (Rom. 6:23).

You may be wondering, *Can't God simply forgive us?* That is a good question, but God would not be just if He did not enact the consequences for our sin. You wouldn't want a human authority to "just forgive" someone who had committed horrible crimes; why should God be any different?

But at the same time, God wants to be with us. He wants to give us life. Though He could not let our sin go unpunished, He did not want to hand over to death the beings He created for eternal life. We've seen this since the beginning of the storyline of Scripture: God has demonstrated His mercy toward His people by offering sacrifices and substitutes to die in their place. In Genesis 3, God covers the shame of Adam and Eve by clothing them with skins from a sacrificial animal. In Genesis 22, Isaac is spared through the offering of a sacrificial ram. Even more than that, the entire sacrificial system established in the Old Testament is based upon the fact that priests would offer sacrifices to God. Specifically, they would offer sacrificial lambs by sprinkling their blood on the altar and mercy seat, the very place that God dwells.

Why all of this death? Why all of this blood? Because the penalty for sin must be paid. The author of Hebrews reminds us, "without the shedding of blood there is no forgiveness" (Heb. 9:22). All this blood and death should serve as a reminder of the seriousness of our sin. But all these sacrificial measures were just temporary. If we are going to be finally, fully, and forever free from sin and rebellion, we don't just need a substitute—we need a specific kind of substitute. If human sins are ever going to be truly forgiven, we need a *human* substitute, while at the same time, if our sins are going to be eternally forgiven, we also need an *eternal* substitute.

Who can fit this bill? Who is both *human* and *eternal* in nature? Only Jesus Christ, the Word in human flesh. It is only through the death of the perfect Son of God that we can be reconciled once and for all (Heb. 10:10).

Our sin against God requires an infinite penalty, so only the infinite One can fully pay it. In the incarnation, the Son of God takes our place. This is why when John the Baptist sees Jesus at His baptism, he says, "Look, the Lamb of God, who takes away the sin of the world!" (John 1:29). We have been bought with the precious blood of Christ, the spotless lamb of God (1 Pet. 1:19).

Because of the life, death, burial, and resurrection of Jesus, God is both just and the justifier (Rom. 3:26). He is the one who entirely maintains His justice by delivering the righteous consequences of sin and rebellion. He is also the justifier because in His mercy, He offers His people a substitute: Jesus Christ.

There is nothing that we could have done to make ourselves right with God. The consequences of our rebellion are simply too much for us to pay. But the good news is we can be the people of God once again, not because of anything we have done, but because of what Christ has done in our place. This is the gospel: not what *we must* do, but what *Christ has* done. Paul reminds the church in Rome of this fact when he says, "God proves his own love for us in that while we were still sinners, Christ died for us" (Rom. 5:8).

Some theologians have called this the "great exchange." Paul appeals to this exchange when he says, "He made the one who did not know sin to be sin for us, so that in him we might become the righteousness of God" (2 Cor. 5:21). This is at the very heart of the storyline of the Bible. The perfect one who knew no sin became sin. The imperfect ones who only know sin can now become the righteousness of God.

God's people can be God's people again. That means sinners can become saints. The unrighteous are counted as righteous. God's enemies are reconciled. Our rebellion is forgiven. Spiritual orphans have been adopted. Those sick with sin have been healed. Those who live in shame receive honor. Those who are enslaved are set free. Those who walked in defeat are now victorious. As God's people, we have received a new identity through Christ's accomplishment in His death and resurrection. God's people, because of the atoning work of Christ, are now:

> **Forgiven:** Though our sin separates us from God, through the death of Christ we are forgiven. "In him we have redemption, the forgiveness of sins" (Col. 1:14).
>
> **Righteous:** "But to the one who does not work, but believes on him who justifies the ungodly, his faith is credited for righteousness" (Rom. 4:5).
>
> **Saved:** "He has saved us and called us with a holy calling, not according to our works, but according to his own purpose and grace, which was given to us in Christ Jesus before time began" (2 Tim. 1:9).

Reconciled: "But now he has reconciled you by his physical body through his death, to present you holy, faultless, and blameless before him" (Col. 1:22).

Justified: "Therefore, since we have been justified by faith, we have peace with God through our Lord Jesus Christ" (Rom. 5:1).

Sanctified: "But you were washed, you were sanctified, you were justified in the name of the Lord Jesus Christ and by the Spirit of our God" (1 Cor. 6:11).

Adopted: "He predestined us to be adopted as sons through Jesus Christ for himself, according to the good pleasure of his will" (Eph. 1:5).

Redeemed: "In him we have redemption through his blood, the forgiveness of our trespasses, according to the riches of his grace" (Eph. 1:7).

Cleansed: "Let us draw near with a true heart in full assurance of faith, with our hearts sprinkled clean from an evil conscience and our bodies washed in pure water" (Heb. 10:22).

Healed: "He himself bore our sins in his body on the tree; so that, having died to

> sins, we might live for righteousness. By his wounds, you have been healed" (1 Pet. 2:24).
>
> **Free:** "But now, since you have been set free from sin and have become enslaved to God, you have your fruit, which results in sanctification—and the outcome is eternal life!" (Rom. 6:22).
>
> **Victorious:** "But thanks be to God, who gives us the victory through our Lord Jesus Christ!" (1 Cor. 15:57).

Isn't that good news? We are declared to be God's people not because of who we are but because of who He is. We are declared the people of God not because of our accomplishments but because of Christ's accomplishments. Our greatest hope in life and death, as an old catechism says, is that we are not our own, but belong to God. God has made us His again.

All of this can be yours by grace through faith. God's people are not identified by socioeconomic status, gender, ethnicity, or intellectual ability. You are not a Christian because of the home you grew up in. You are not part of the people of God because of your political beliefs or who you voted for in the last election. The only way to be counted among Christ's people is through faith in King Jesus. Paul writes, "For you are saved by grace through faith, and this is not from yourselves; it is God's gift—not from works, so that no one can boast"

(Eph. 2:8–9). The good news about King Jesus is that He is full of grace. There is more mercy in Christ than there is sin in us. You can be a recipient of God's covenantal mercy by simply trusting Christ as the fulfillment of all of God's promises. Our salvation begins with grace, is sustained by grace, and will be completed by grace, through faith.

Every single one of God's covenants to His people is a reminder that God has been faithful to us in Christ. That is why Paul says, "For every one of God's promises is 'Yes' in him" (2 Cor. 1:20). Christ fulfills all the kingdom covenants.

In Christ, God was faithful to send the Son born of a woman who crushes the head of the serpent at Golgotha.

In Christ, God was faithful to send the Son, born of a woman, who is the Son of Abraham who offers a sacrifice that blesses the nations.

In Christ, God was faithful to send the Son of David, who in His life, death, burial, and resurrection establishes a kingdom without end.

In Christ, God was faithful to pour out His Holy Spirit after the ascension so that the church may be the tabernacling presence of God.

In Christ, God has begun to restore His kingdom to this world.

Remember and Rehearse

Remember the cross.

One of the most important things you can do as you seek to combat the false stories you live in is remember the cross of Jesus Christ. At the cross, Jesus accomplished everything necessary for salvation, and it's yours by faith. Perhaps you struggle with perfectionism, believing that you can somehow make yourself righteous before God. Maybe you struggle with romanticism, believing that God only loves you to the extent that you can feel it. Maybe you struggle with politicalism, believing that the kingdoms of this world are our hope. The antidote to all of our false stories is the cross of Jesus Christ. None of our false stories can comprehend the magnitude of God's love for us in Christ.

As we remember the life, death, and burial of Christ, we are invited to fight our false stories the same way that Paul did by proclaiming, "I have been crucified with Christ, and I no longer live, but Christ lives in me. The life I now live in the body, I live by faith in the Son of God, who loved me and gave himself for me" (Gal. 2:20). This is an example of Paul warring against his false story. He is remembering that the cross of Jesus Christ is where all of our false stories go to die. Now Christ is powerfully alive in us by faith. The primary way we fight against the false narratives of our world is by pointing ourselves and all people to the person and work of Jesus Christ.

Rehearse the gospel by living cross-shaped lives.

As we seek to live in the true story of the world, we can rehearse the good news of the gospel by being the kind of people who are marked by cross-shaped—or cruciform—lives. Don't forget when Jesus asked Peter who he said Jesus was, Jesus did not simply tell him and His other disciples that He was going to go to the cross. He also told them that they would carry their own crosses. We rehearse the good news of the gospel when we follow Jesus as His disciples by carrying our own crosses. Jesus tells His disciples,

> "If anyone wants to follow after me, let him deny himself, take up his cross, and follow me. For whoever wants to save his life will lose it, but whoever loses his life because of me will find it. For what will it benefit someone if he gains the whole world yet loses his life? Or what will anyone give in exchange for his life?" (Matt. 16:24–26)

So many of us desire comfort, but Jesus calls us to our cross. Every single one of our false stories is confronted by the cross of Jesus Christ, and as His disciples, we rehearse the kingdom when we carry them.

Summary

The gospel of the kingdom is the good news that Christ has come to establish the kingdom of God. The story of the Bible finds its fulfillment in the person and work of Jesus Christ. He is the promised Son who comes to bring the kingdom through the new covenant in His life, death, burial, resurrection, and ascension.

Discussion Questions

1. How would you tell the story of the kingdom of God culminating in the person and work of Jesus Christ? How does His ministry, His life, and His death on the cross all point to the kingdom of God?

2. Can you trace the way Jesus fulfills all the other covenants? How did creation point to Him? How did the covenant with Abraham point to Him? The covenant with Moses? The covenant with David? The covenant in exile?

3. What does it mean to remember the cross each day? How might your life be different today if you remembered the cross and rehearsed the gospel by living a cross-shaped life?

CHAPTER 11

The Spirit and the Church: The King and His People

On Saturday, May 6, 2023, the world's attention was on Westminster Abbey in London as people across the globe watched the coronation of the first British monarch in almost seventy years. King Charles III was crowned king shortly after the death of his mother, Queen Elizabeth II.

In moments like this, we are reminded that civilizations have, for centuries, celebrated the enthronement and coordination of their kings and queens. Once a king or queen is enthroned and crowned, they are able to bestow all the benefits of the kingdom upon their citizens.

The last chapter considered how the person of Jesus Christ and His death on the cross brings about the fulfillment of everything God promised to His people. For a lot of people, this is where their understanding of the gospel stops. They believe the good news of the gospel is that Jesus Christ died on the cross for their sin.

But the Bible tells us a very different story. The good news of the gospel is not that Jesus Christ simply died on the cross, but that He was buried, rose again, ascended into heaven, and now grants us all the benefits of salvation by sending His Holy Spirit.

When we place our faith in Christ, we are not placing our faith in a dead king. We are placing our faith in the true King who has triumphed over Satan, sin, and death. The Gospels do not end with the death of Christ, but with His resurrection and the announcement of His victory in the resurrection.

INCARNATION:
The Son existing in the form of God empties Himself to the point of death on a cross.

RESURRECTION AND ASCENSION:
For this reason, God highly exalted Him and gave Him the name that is above every name.

Each Gospel writer provides a slightly different perspective on the story of Christ's resurrection, but all of them proclaim the good news that Christ has risen from the dead (Matt. 28:6; Mark 16:6; Luke 24:6; John 20:16–17). In John's account, we get a picture of Mary Magdalene looking desperately for her crucified and dead friend. She arrived at the tomb early in the morning only to see that the stone had been removed from the tomb (John 20:1). She is overwhelmed with grief, believing someone stole His body.

Mary stays outside the tomb, crying, and has an interaction with a man that she does not recognize. She assumes He is the gardener (John 20:15). I don't think that is an accident. In this account we see the entire story of the Bible in just a few paragraphs. The man she presumes to be the gardener speaks with His northern Galilean voice and says her name, *Mary*. The man she thinks is the gardener turns out to be Jesus. She cries out in Aramaic, "Rabboni" which means teacher (John 20:16).

Jesus is the true gardener, having emerged victorious from the dirt of the grave. The first gardener, Adam, turned the garden into a grave. The second gardener, Christ, turns the grave into a garden. The first gardener, Adam, was taken up out of the dirt and given life, but returns to the dirt because of his sin. The second gardener, Christ, was put in the dirt for our sin, but emerged from it victoriously, granting us salvation.

The despair of death that humanity has lived with since Eden has now been defeated by the resurrected king. In the resurrection of Christ, we see the very beginning of God's cosmic renewal of all of creation. Christ has taken on the consequence of death, but has fully, finally, and forever defeated it.

The gospel is not simply that Jesus died. That is not good news by itself. If Christ has not been raised, our faith is worthless and we are still in our sins (1 Cor. 15:14). The good news of the gospel is that Jesus died and rose again, defeating death. The message of resurrection is that God's mission of kingdom restoration has now been accomplished and revealed by Jesus Christ, and we are invited to be participants in it.

After His resurrection, the earthly ministry of Jesus continues proclaiming the good news of the kingdom of God as He spends forty days with His people. He gives His disciples a Bible reading lesson on the road to Emmaus, telling them that the entire storyline of Scripture is about Him, His death, and His resurrection (Luke 24:27, 46–49). He also commissions His disciples for work in this kingdom, telling them:

> "Go, therefore, and make disciples of all nations, baptizing them in the name of the Father and of the Son and of the Holy Spirit, teaching them to observe everything I have commanded you. And remember, I am with

> you always, to the end of the age." (Matt. 28:19–20)

The kingdom is still the only talking point for the resurrected King.

Jesus Ascends and Sends the Holy Spirit

Even after His resurrection, the ministry of King Jesus continues. Sometimes referred to as the "forgotten" act of Jesus, He ascends into heaven. This is an essential element of the gospel because our King wasn't just crucified. Our King wasn't just resurrected. Our King currently reigns from His throne in heaven.

In the ascension, the Son of David has taken His rightful place at the right hand of the Father, where He reigns and rules from an eternal heavenly throne (Acts 2:29–36). Jesus was enthroned as King at the cross, and He was crowned as King in His ascension. The crucified King is now forever crowned as Lord.

Paul highlights the permanent and eternal kingship of Jesus and the ascension when he claims,

> He exercised this power in Christ by raising him from the dead and seating him at his right hand in the heavens—far above every ruler and authority, power and dominion,

> and every title given, not only in this age but also in the one to come. And he subjected everything under his feet, and appointed him as head over everything for the church, which is his body, the fullness of the one who fills all things in every way. (Eph 1:20–23)

Paul also connects the humility of Christ in His death to the victory of Christ in His ascension when he writes to the Philippian church. He argues,

> He humbled himself by becoming obedient to the point of death—even to death on a cross. For this reason God highly exalted him and gave him the name that is above every name, so that at the name of Jesus every knee will bow—in heaven and on earth and under the earth—and every tongue will confess that Jesus Christ is Lord, to the glory of God the Father. (Phil. 2:8–11)

For the New Testament, the crucifixion, resurrection, and ascension of Christ is meant to be viewed as one event—all about the re-establishment of the kingdom. The king suffers, dies, is buried, resurrects, and ascends to reign and rule over all things.

After His ascension, Jesus does not simply kick His feet up and rest. He is currently reigning and ruling in power from His throne. It is good news the tomb is empty, but it is also good news the throne is occupied. King Jesus is alive and well, joyfully extending His kingdom to all tribes, tongues, and peoples. He is not anxious. He is not concerned about His kingdom plans. He doesn't fret about the future. He has not neglected His people. King Jesus is alive and at work, dispensing His Holy Spirit on dead people, making them alive. Every time a person becomes a Christian, our resurrected and ascended King continues to establish and extend the kingdom of God through the person and work of the Holy Spirit.

God eternally exists as one God in three distinct persons: God the Father, God the Son, and God the Holy Spirit. After the ascension, God the Father and God the Son send the Holy Spirit to continue the work of the kingdom. The Spirit comes to apply all the benefits of King Jesus to His people and to establish and extend the gospel of the kingdom to the whole world.

After His ascension, the crucified King sends the Holy Spirit to:

- Indwell us with God's Personal **Presence**.
- Create God's **People**—the church.

- Empower us as we live out God's **Purpose** of the Great Commandment and the Great Commission.
- Reclaim the entire world as God's **Place**.

The Holy Spirit: God's Personal Presence

After His ascension, the first act of Christ is to breathe out the Holy Spirit on His people. The Holy Spirit is sent to indwell us with God's Personal **Presence**.

This should not come as a surprise. When Jesus was in the Upper Room with His disciples before His death, He told them, "It is for your benefit that I go away, because if I don't go away the Counselor will not come to you. If I go, I will send him to you" (John 16:7). Jesus's disciples are those who should eagerly anticipate the presence of God in their lives.

John even shows us that right after His resurrection, Jesus's very first act—even before His ascension—is to offer His disciples the Holy Spirit. In Genesis 2:7, God forms man from the dust and "breathed the breath of life into his nostrils, and the man became a living being." In John 20:22 Jesus breathes on His disciples and says, "Receive the Holy Spirit."

The same God who is in the garden with Adam and Eve, giving them the breath of life, now breathes out His Holy Spirit in His people, as we see in Acts 2:

> When the day of Pentecost had arrived, they were all together in one place. Suddenly a sound like that of a violent rushing wind came from heaven, and it filled the whole house where they were staying. They saw tongues like flames of fire that separated and rested on each one of them. Then they were all filled with the Holy Spirit and began to speak in different tongues, as the Spirit enabled them. (Acts 2:1–4)

God is now personally present, not just *with*, but *in* His people.

The tongues of fire serve as a reminder of God's covenants. The same God who once appeared as fire and smoke to walk down a bloody aisle to make a covenant with Abraham is with us. The same God who appeared in a burning bush with Moses is with us. The same God who led God's people in the wilderness with a pillar of fire is with us. The same God whose glory filled Solomon's temple is with us. The Holy Spirit is with us as the covenant-keeping God.

When Jesus breathes out His Holy Spirit, He initiates the project that is reserved for the King—temple building. But King Jesus is not building a temple made out of stone or mortar. Instead, King Jesus is building a temple made up of people. The Son of David is promised by God that He will build an eternal temple, and that is exactly what Jesus begins to do when He ascends to the Father (2 Sam. 7:13).

When writing to the Corinthian church, the apostle Paul reminded them that they are the dwelling place of God. "Don't you yourselves know that you are God's temple and that the Spirit of God lives in you?" (1 Cor. 3:16). Sometimes what is missed in this verse is that Paul is not only addressing individuals, but the entire church. In other words, to use a Texas translation: "*Y'all* are God's temple."

This imagery is really quite stunning when we consider it in the context of the storyline of Scripture. He is saying that God's people, in fulfillment of the New Covenant made in exile, are now the house of God. God's people no longer need to go to a building to experience the presence of God, but God has come to them and taken up residence in them.

He goes on to highlight not only that God indwells the entire church corporately, but each of the members individually, "Don't you know that your body is a temple of the Holy Spirit who is in you, whom you have from God? You are not your own, for you were bought at a price. So glorify God with your body" (1 Cor. 6:19–20).

When Jesus Christ sends the Holy Spirit to His people, we know that He is bringing about an end to our exile. Jesus Christ has not just extended forgiveness to us; He is also extending the presence of God to us. Our exile will one day be over forever, and we have the guarantee of that promise now in the Holy Spirit.

The Church: God's People

In His ascension, the king is also recreating a kingdom people for Himself: the church.

The primary distinguishing feature of the people of God is the presence of God. God's people are not identified by nationality, socioeconomic status, ethnicity, or intellectual ability. The people of God are primarily identified by the fact that God dwells in us.

But how do we become a member of God's household? We have to be born into this new family through the work of the Holy Spirit. That is what Jesus tells Nicodemus in John 3.

Nicodemus comes to Jesus inquiring how Jesus is performing His miracles. Jesus tells him, "Truly I tell you, unless someone is born again, he cannot see the kingdom of God" (John 3:3). The kingdom is not inherited through natural birth, but through spiritual rebirth.

Nicodemus, still confused, asks Jesus how that is even possible. How can someone be born again? Jesus responds, "Truly I tell you, unless someone is born of water and the Spirit, he cannot enter the kingdom of God. Whatever is born of the flesh is flesh, and whatever is born of the Spirit is spirit. Do not be amazed that I told you that you must be born again. The wind blows where it pleases, and you hear its sound, but you don't know where it comes from or where it is going. So it is with everyone born of the Spirit" (John 3:5–8). Ezekiel prophesied that one day dry bones would be revived (see Ezek. 37:5–6). The Holy Spirit comes to grant God's people new life as those who are born of Him.

That means God's people find their primary identities not in their natural birth, or in the things of this world, but in their spiritual birth, granted to them by the Holy Spirit.

Nicodemus still questions how this could be true. Jesus responds,

> "Just as Moses lifted up the snake in the wilderness, so the Son of Man must be lifted up, so that everyone who believes in him may have eternal life. For God loved the world in this way: He gave his one and only Son, so that everyone who believes in him will not perish but have eternal life." (John 3:14–16)

Whoever believes in Christ and His gospel is granted eternal life. That means we gain access to the family of God by being born again through the Holy Spirit, which is received and granted only through faith. John already mentioned this briefly in His introduction. He tells us, "But to all who did receive him, he gave them the right to be children of God, to those who believe in his name, who were born, not of natural descent, or of the will of the flesh, or of the will of man, but of God" (John 1:12–13).

It is only through faith that we are adopted into the family of God—and *family* is an appropriate reality to consider for the people of God. Throughout the New Testament, God's people are referred to with familial language—as brothers and sisters. The family of God now incorporates anybody who confesses the good news of the gospel by faith. In the New Testament, we see all kinds of different people grafted into God's family as brothers and sisters. Roman slaves, Pharisees, Samaritans, Roman officials, Jews, and many more are incorporated into Christ's new family, the church. Just consider Paul's final goodbye to the church in Romans 16. In that chapter we see an unbelievably diverse group of men and women: Phoebe, a servant of the church in Cenchreae; Priscilla and Aquila co-laborers with Paul; Andronicus and Junia, fellow Jews, and fellow prisoners; Ampliatus and Urbanus, friends and coworkers of Paul; Tertius and Quartus, likely Romans slaves; Gaius, a man of means who is hosting Paul and Erastus, the city treasurer.

There is nothing in this world that could have brought these people together. On earth, they share almost nothing in common; but in Christ, they share the most important thing in common. Christ has called them from all walks of life and backgrounds, and He has brought them into His new kingdom family.

In the world, there would have been far too many things that separated these groups of people. But now, they share something far more important in common: the blood of Jesus Christ.

One of the essential ministries of the Holy Spirit is not just to draw people into God's new family, but to also sanctify them—that is, to make them holy. The ministry of the Holy Spirit is to apply all that Christ has accomplished. Christ has not only accomplished our justification—that we have been made right with God. The Holy Spirit also applies our sanctification—that we are invited to grow in holiness through His power.

We read in 1 Peter 2:9, "But you are a chosen race, a royal priesthood, a holy nation, a people for his possession." The good news of the gospel is not just that we have been forgiven, but that we are being made holy. God's Spirit does not just come to make dead people alive. He also comes to make sinful people holy. The Holy Spirit frees us from the enslavement of sin and invites us into joyful obedience to Christ, "for the kingdom of God is not eating and drinking, but righteousness, peace, and joy in the Holy Spirit" (Rom. 14:17).

The Holy Spirit, given to God's people, can never be revoked. The Spirit is God with us forever. Paul argues,

> In him you also were sealed with the promised Holy Spirit when you heard the word

> of truth, the gospel of your salvation, and when you believed. The Holy Spirit is the down payment of our inheritance, until the redemption of the possession, to the praise of his glory. (Eph 1:13–14)

Once sealed, always sealed. The Holy Spirit is the unbreakable bond by which King Jesus united us to Himself and His kingdom.

The Great Commandment and Commission: God's Purpose

The Holy Spirit, God's personal presence, is now alive in us in order to empower God's people to live out God's **Purpose:** the Great Commandment and the Great Commission.

Toward the end of Jesus's earthly ministry, the Pharisees and the Sadducees were still trying to trap Him, showing the crowds that He was a false teacher. One of them came to ask Him a question in order to test Him. He asked Jesus, "Which command in the law is the greatest?" Jesus responds, "Love the Lord your God with all your heart, with all your soul, and with all your mind. This is the greatest and most important command. The second is like it: Love your neighbor as yourself. All the Law and the Prophets depend on these two commands" (Matt. 22:36–40).

In just a few words, Jesus distills the entirety of the law and prophets into two commands:

> Love God with everything.
>
> Love your neighbor as yourself.

In some sense, He is pointing our attention back to the original cultural mandate found in Genesis 1:26–28 to bring glory to God by loving Him and extending His dominion to all of creation. Despite the simplicity of these commands, they are unbelievably challenging. Jesus frames these commands as affections of the heart. The commands of Christ are based upon love.

But ever since sin entered the world, our affections have been distorted. Rather than loving God, we love other things. Rather than loving our neighbors, we love ourselves.

That is why Jesus sends the Holy Spirit into the church and into our lives. The presence of the Holy Spirit empowers us to love God and our neighbors. This should remind us of what Jeremiah promised the exiles about the new covenant. As a reminder, Jeremiah promises God's people in exile that a day is coming when,

> "I will put my teaching within them and write it on their hearts. I will be their God, and they will be my people. No longer will one teach his neighbor or his brother, saying,

> 'Know the Lord,' for they will all know me, from the least to the greatest of them"—this is the Lord's declaration. "For I will forgive their iniquity and never again remember their sin." (Jer. 31:33–34)

When you receive the Holy Spirit by faith, He begins to empower you to live according to God's law. Why? Because God's teaching is now within you, written on your heart. This does not mean that all of our internal inclinations should be followed. On the contrary, we are invited to no longer live according to the flesh, but according to the Spirit (Gal. 5). We no longer only have God's law externally, but now internally, and the Holy Spirit empowers and enables genuine obedience to God.

Jesus tells His disciples that this purpose of God—obedience to His law—will be empowered and enabled by the gift of the Holy Spirit. He tells them, "If you love me, you will keep my commands. And I will ask the Father, and he will give you another Counselor, to be with you forever. He is the Spirit of truth. The world is unable to receive him because it doesn't see him or know him. But you do know him, because he remains with you and will be in you" (John 14:15–17). God does not simply demand obedience—He empowers it. Left to ourselves, we would live in the flesh. But through receiving the Spirit, obedience to God's law is now possible.

Paul, writing to the church in Galatia, invites them to live according to the Spirit, rather than the flesh. He says,

> But the fruit of the Spirit is love, joy, peace, patience, kindness, goodness, faithfulness, gentleness, and self-control. The law is not against such things. Now those who belong to Christ Jesus have crucified the flesh with its passions and desires. If we live by the Spirit, let us also keep in step with the Spirit. (Gal. 5:22–25)

It is impossible to live according to the purposes of God without the Spirit.

But not only does Jesus invite His disciples into obedience through the Spirit, He also commissions us as missionaries. Immediately before His ascension, He gives final marching orders to His disciples,

> "All authority has been given to me in heaven and on earth. Go, therefore, and make disciples of all nations, baptizing them in the name of the Father and of the Son and of the Holy Spirit, teaching them to observe everything I have commanded you. And remember, I am with you always, to the end of the age." (Matt. 28:18–20)

Jesus tells His disciples that He is King. All authority has been given to Him, in heaven and on earth.

Jesus tells His disciples to go and make more disciples of all nations.

Jesus tells His disciples to give people a new identity through baptism in the triune name.

Jesus tells His disciples to teach everything He has commanded.

How is all of this possible? Because Jesus Christ, through His Spirit, is with us to the end of the age. Not only does Jesus commission His church to make disciples, He empowers their mission through the presence of the Holy Spirit. Because of the gift of the Holy Spirit, we are now invited to live in the purposes of God. We can love God with everything we have. We can love our neighbors as ourselves. We can make disciples of Jesus Christ.

The World: God's Place

King Jesus, through the Spirit-empowered church, is reclaiming the entire world as God's **Place**.

Immediately before His ascension, Jesus encourages His disciples, "But you will receive power when the Holy Spirit has come on you, and you will be my witnesses in Jerusalem, in all Judea and Samaria, and *to the ends of the earth*" (Acts 1:8, emphasis mine).

This was potentially very confusing for His disciples. They were probably thinking the King and His kingdom belonged in Jerusalem. God is present in Jerusalem. God's people are in Jerusalem. God's purposes will be lived out in Jerusalem. God's place is Jerusalem. That's how it was in the older covenants—that's how it should be now, right?

But Jesus tells His disciples that the empowering witness of the Holy Spirit is to not only be witnesses in Jerusalem, but to be witnesses in all of Judea, and even in Samaria, and yes, that's right, even to the ends of the earth.

The mission of God is never content to stay in one place. The mission of God is an expanding mission to all peoples and all places. That's because God's place is not restricted to a city. God's place is cosmic. Everything belongs to Him, and through the Holy Spirit, He is reclaiming all of His creation.

This is exactly what we see the early church begin to participate in. Throughout the book of Acts, we see the Holy Spirit expanding God's place to previously unthinkable places.

The Holy Spirit is poured out on the church in Jerusalem on the Day of Pentecost, but things don't stop there. Soon after the establishment of the church, persecution comes. Stephen preaches the gospel in Jerusalem and as a result, becomes the first Christian martyr (Acts 7:54–60). After his death, a severe persecution came upon the church, forcing them out of Jerusalem into other regions.

Because of this persecution, the church begins to witness in other regions. We read in Acts 9:31, "So the church throughout all Judea, Galilee, and Samaria had peace and was strengthened. Living in the fear of the Lord and encouraged by the Holy Spirit, it increased in numbers."

The disciples begin to realize that this mission is no longer simply for Jews, but also Gentiles—that is, for all the nations. God does not simply desire for His presence to be in Jerusalem, but also in places like Caesarea, where a man named Cornelius has a vision, leading to many Gentile conversions. Peter realizes that God does not favor people or places, but that He desires for all people in all places to know Him.

This leads the church to witness, evangelize, and plant churches in new places. Again, these places and regions were shocking to the early church. The earliest disciples had to transition their thinking from believing that God's presence was meant to be in Jerusalem to understanding that God's presence belongs in all of creation. So they begin planting churches in places like Antioch, Iconium, Lystra, Thessalonica, Athens, Corinth, Ephesus, Troas, Macedonia, Miletus, Rome, Spain, all over Europe, and eventually to the ends of the earth.

It was this vision that all peoples and places belong to God that was the fuel for Paul's church planting ministry. His three missionary journeys took decades of his life and forced him to travel more than 10,000 miles. Consider how challenging that would have been in his day. All of these miles were covered by Paul and his associates on foot, on the back of an animal, or in the hull of a ship. There was no engine. There were no airplanes. There was no convenient way for Paul and the early church to extend the mission of God to all places. But through the power of the Holy Spirit, they knew God's mission was not restricted to a temple in Jerusalem—that the place of God was meant to be extended to the whole world.

Where are you reading this book right now? Perhaps you are sitting in a coffee shop somewhere in the United States of America. Maybe you are reading this in a library somewhere in Europe. Perhaps you are reading this as a part of a Bible study in Australia. Maybe you are reading this with your church in Africa. Regardless of where you are, I want you to take a moment and ponder the expansive mission of God. This mission that began with a few disciples in Jerusalem has come to you, and it is still extending and expanding to the ends of the earth. Why? Because all people and all places belong to Him.

Praise God for this expansive mission and thank God for the empowering work of the Holy Spirit to fuel the mission and witness of Christ's church. When the church is sent out on mission, we don't always know where Jesus will take us, but we have assurance that He will always be with us.

Remember and Rehearse

Remember the gift of the Spirit in the church.

The primary way the Holy Spirit indwells the church of Jesus Christ combats the false stories of the world is through gathering together for corporate worship. Do not underestimate the importance of your local church and how that local church helps you resist the false stories of the world.

One of the primary responsibilities of every local church is to help its members live in the true story of the world. You could make the case that every single time the local church gathers together is an opportunity to re-story God's people. Every Sunday morning is an invitation to remember and rehearse the true story of the Bible.

Rehearse the future events in the kingdom of God in corporate worship with the church.

In corporate worship, we remember who God is by singing about His holiness, by worshipping Him for His transcendence, by reminding each other of His glory. In corporate worship, we are invited to remember our brokenness and sinfulness by confessing our sins to God and to each other. And in corporate worship, we are invited to sit under the preached Word of God, that the Holy Spirit enlivens. When God's

Word is proclaimed, the mission of God goes forward in our lives and in the world. The proclaimed Word is a refutation of all the false stories of the world and an invitation to live in the storyline of Scripture.

In corporate worship we are invited to the waters of baptism. We are reminded that just like at the waters of the Red Sea, the waters of Jordan, or the waters of baptism, God invites His people to die to themselves and to live in Him. Baptism is a reminder that all who are in Christ have been buried with Him in baptism. And if we have been united with Him in baptism, we will also be united with Him in His resurrection. Not only is baptism a reminder that we have died to ourselves, it is also a rehearsal of the future kingdom of God—that one day we will be resurrected with Christ into the kingdom of God.

In corporate worship, we are invited to participate in the Lord's Supper. When Jesus offered this meal to His disciples, He told them that this meal was an opportunity to remember Him. He tells them to eat the bread and drink the cup "in remembrance" of Him (Luke 22:19). But He also tells them that He will not participate in this meal again, "until the kingdom of God comes" (v. 18). Every single time the church gathers together, we are looking back in remembrance and rehearsing with anticipation. We are invited to look back and remember all that God has done as we hear His Word proclaimed, as we celebrate baptism, and as we receive the Lord's

Supper. In each of these events, we are invited to remember God's faithfulness to us.

The church gathered is the community that remembers and rehearses together. The church is the primary place that God's people, indwelt by the Holy Spirit, remember and rehearse the past and future events of the kingdom of God. That means, Christian, that you should prioritize church attendance. It is hard to overestimate the importance of the local church.

We can be re-storied as we join a local church that proclaims the gospel.

We can be re-storied as we enjoy and delight in the proclamation of that gospel every single week through God's Word.

We can be re-storied as we celebrate baptisms in the local church. Look back at your baptism and be reminded that you have died to who you were and you are now alive in Christ.

We can be re-storied at the Lord's Table, as we remember who Jesus is and what He's accomplished. Rehearse the feast you will have with Him in the future.

We can be re-storied as we live on mission. Evangelize the lost. Plant new churches. Serve in kids ministry. Care for orphans and widows. Participate in Christ's kingdom community now.

Summary

After His resurrection and ascension, Jesus sends the Holy Spirit to apply all the benefits of salvation. The Holy Spirit indwells the people of God by applying the blessings of the King and forming the kingdom community.

Discussion Questions

1. How would you tell the story of how the ascension of Christ and the gift of the Spirit empower God's people to be citizens of the kingdom of God?

2. How did this chapter change your perspective on what Jesus is doing right now?

3. What is your background or experience with conversations about the Holy Spirit? Did this chapter change your view at all?

4. How have you seen God's character through the work of the Spirit in His people in the church?

5. Why does corporate worship matter?

CHAPTER 12

Kingdom without End: The Coming of the King

One of the most important elements to any story is how it begins—something we've already explored. But equally important is how the story ends. An ending can make or break a story.

A good ending is meant to remind you of the beginning. Let's remember together how the story of Scripture began. The storyline of the Bible begins with the establishment of God's kingdom. In a garden paradise, God sets up His kingdom.

- God is **present** with His creation.
- God forms a **people**, image-bearers, for Himself.

- God establishes a **place** for His kingdom to reside.
- God grants His people the **purpose** of giving Him glory and extending His kingdom to all of creation.

Christ Will Come Again

Different Christian communities have different views on the end times—or the precise details of how things will wrap up. Some Christian communities over-prioritize their interpretation of these details and get hung up talking about the when, where, and how, while other Christian communities have instead been so hesitant to talk about the end times that they tend to neglect it altogether.

What I hope to do in this chapter is to invite you to consider the end of the story in light of the beginning, which means it is all about the coming kingdom. Instead of debating the secondary issues, I'd rather focus on the essential hope that all Christians share in common: the coming of the King and His kingdom.

Maybe you've been hesitant to consider how the story ends because you find it all a bit unnerving, maybe you've put too much focus on this in the past, or maybe this is all new to you. No matter where you are coming from, you are invited to live your life in light of the end. Today we are invited to live kingdom-shaped lives of great expectancy, joy, and anticipation. Why? Because the end of the Bible is the best ending to any story you've ever read.

The King is coming to fulfill His kingdom-covenants to His people.

In Genesis 1–2 we read the story of a kingdom established. In Revelation 21–22 we read the story of a kingdom reestablished forever. In some sense, the Bible begins where it ends. In the final two chapters of the Bible, we read a mirror reflection of the first two. At the beginning of Scripture, and at the end, the message is simple: God is establishing His kingdom on earth forever.

In Revelation 21–22 we receive the good news that:

- God's **presence** will be with us forever.
- God's **people** will belong to Him forever.
- God's **place** will endure forever.
- God's **purposes** will prosper forever.

God's presence will be with us forever.

The story of Scripture from beginning to end places a priority on the presence of God with His people. God was present with His people in the garden of Eden, and God has been working to end our exile since Genesis 3.

Throughout the story, God has been so merciful to give us His presence. He met with Abraham. He spoke with Moses from the burning bush. He guided His people in the wilderness. He dwelt in the midst of His people in the temple and in the tabernacle. In the incarnation, He dwelt with us in Christ. With the sending of the Spirit, He dwells in us personally. The entire story, to this point, is about God with us.

But the story doesn't end with the sending of the Spirit to the church. Paul calls the indwelling presence of the Spirit a "down payment of our inheritance, until the redemption of the possession" (Eph. 1:14). Paul uses this language because the gift of the Spirit is a foretaste of the coming experience of God's presence. The Spirit's presence with us is real, but it also is intended to make us desire God's presence even more. The end of the story tells us that one day the King will bring His kingdom, ending our exile forever. At the end of the story the presence of God isn't just in us; the manifest presence of God is everywhere.

That is exactly what we read at the beginning of Revelation 21. The apostle John tells us,

> Then I saw a new heaven and a new earth; for the first heaven and the first earth had passed away, and the sea was no more. I also saw the holy city, the new Jerusalem, coming down out of heaven from God, prepared

> like a bride adorned for her husband. Then
> I heard a loud voice from the throne: Look,
> God's dwelling is with humanity. (vv. 1–3)

Doesn't the end of the story remind you of the beginning? God dwelling with His people in the kingdom.

In this passage John points out the direction of our hope. Our exile does not end because we eventually find our way to God, but because God comes to rescue us. The entire point of Scripture's storyline is not that we escape this world, but that God brings salvation and restoration to this world.

Our hope isn't that we go to the kingdom. Our hope is that the kingdom comes to us.

We don't go home. Home comes to us.

Do you remember what happened immediately after Jesus's ascension? Two angels appeared to the disciples and said to them, "Men of Galilee, why do you stand looking up into heaven? This same Jesus, who has been taken from you into heaven, will come in the same way that you have seen him going into heaven" (Acts 1:11). They told the disciples that the victorious King would come back for His people one day.

The King declares that our exile is over. He declares that God is back and is here to stay with us forever. When God's people were in exile, the prophet Habakkuk reminded them that one day "the earth will be filled with the knowledge of the LORD's glory, as the water covers the sea" (Hab. 2:14). This is fulfilled in the vision of God, what is to come in the new heaven and earth. God's presence will be everywhere. The same way water covers the sea.

Peter tells God's people that even though the Spirit indwells them, they are still in exile. He calls God's people "chosen," as those "living as exiles" (1 Pet. 1:1). The Spirit dwells in us, but our future hope is that one day the presence of God will be with us everywhere.

God's people will belong to Him forever.

When King Jesus returns, He will declare our exile is over forever. Christ sets His people free by His blood (Rev. 1:5–6), and because He sets us free He also declares we are His people (Rev. 21:3).

The mission of the church, given by Christ, is to go and make disciples of all nations. Christ sent His church, with the Spirit to testify to the good news of the gospel to all people. At the end of the story, we see that the mission of the Spirit and the church will be successful.

God's people have been made "a kingdom and priests to our God, and they will reign on the earth" (Rev. 5:10).

John tells us,

> After this I looked, and there was a vast multitude from every nation, tribe, people, and language, which no one could number, standing before the throne and before the Lamb. They were clothed in white robes with palm branches in their hands. And they cried out in a loud voice: "Salvation belongs to our God, who is seated on the throne, and to the Lamb!" (Rev. 7:9–10)

The vision that John receives shows us that the King has redeemed His people from all peoples. His mission has been a wonderful success—more so than we could have ever hoped or dreamed, and more so than it sometimes feels.

Today, the nations rage against each other. We live in a world of turmoil, war, and disease. Christ's victory sometimes seems far away. But the mission of the church goes forward, and one day the church will gather around the throne of Christ and worship. People from every nation, tribe, people, and language will stand in robes of righteousness worshipping the slaughtered Lamb who died to save them. The primary identification of God's people at the end is not what language they speak. It's not what country they lived in. It's not how much money they made. It is none of those things. It is simply that we will belong to Him.

He calls us His own—His treasured possession. If you are in Christ, you belong to God forever, and those who belong to Him will suffer no more. Since the fall, God's people have endured the consequences of their sin and sojourned in a broken world. When Christ brings the kingdom, every single consequence and curse will be vanquished forever. John tells us that Christ, "will wipe away every tear from their eyes. Death will be no more; grief, crying, and pain will be no more, because the previous things have passed away" (Rev. 21:4).

RETURN OF CHRIST:
Jesus returns to establish His kingdom and abolish death forever (1 Cor. 15).

RESURRECTION OF THE DEAD:
Those in Christ given everlasting resurrection life.

Sin, gone. Funerals, done away with. Cancer wards, a thing of the past. Bandages, casts, wheelchairs—who needs those? A day is coming when we won't even need a tissue to wipe our tears because the strong and tender hand of Christ will wipe away every last one of them.

How can this be? Because death will finally be defeated, once and for all. Death will die. When Christ returns, He will raise His people in resurrection and they will be victorious over the grave (Rev. 20:1–4). For those in Christ, there is no such thing as a final resting place, only temporary ones. Our future is life everlasting.

This is why Paul calls Christ's resurrection the firstfruits. He argues,

> But as it is, Christ has been raised from the dead, the firstfruits of those who have fallen asleep. For since death came through a man, the resurrection of the dead also comes through a man. For just as in Adam all die, so also in Christ all will be made alive. (1 Cor. 15:20–22)

Christ is the firstfruits because the only thing unique about Jesus's resurrection is that He got to go first. All who die in Christ will emerge in the same way that He did. Why? Because we are God's people. We have been united to Him in Christ. And if we have been united with Him in a death like His, we will also be united with Him in His resurrection (Rom. 6:1–4).

This future promise that is fulfilled in Jesus Christ is the hope that Ezekiel gave God's people. He said, "I will make a covenant of peace with them; it will be a permanent covenant with them. I will establish and multiply them and will set my sanctuary among them forever. My dwelling place will be with them; I will be their God, and they will be my people" (Ezek. 37:26–27).

In addition to God claiming a people for Himself, all of those who do not have faith in Christ will experience eternal separation and judgment from God forever (Rev. 21:8). God's people inherit the kingdom not because of what they've done, but because of what Christ has accomplished on their behalf. All people are invited to freely believe and receive the benefits of the King.

God's people belong to God. We don't belong to ourselves. We don't belong to death. We don't belong to suffering. We don't belong to grief. We belong to God. The King has claimed us as His own. We are His possession, and He will never lose us.

God's place will be restored forever.

Since the beginning, image-bearers have been given the responsibility to take dominion of all of God's creation. Adam and Eve were charged with filling the earth and subduing it (Gen. 1:28). The entire earth was created by God as His dwelling place, and humanity is meant to extend His glory to every square inch of it.

Ever since the fall, God's people have been searching for the land that God has given them. At the end of the story, we see that God still intends to spread His kingdom to the ends of the earth.

Not only will God's kingdom be restored forever, but in addition to that, the rival kingdom Babylon, along with its false stories, will be destroyed forever, "It has fallen, Babylon the Great has fallen!" (Rev. 18:2).

When the New Jerusalem descends out of heaven, we are told by John,

> The one who spoke with me had a golden measuring rod to measure the city, its gates, and its wall. The city is laid out in a square; its length and width are the same. He measured the city with the rod at 12,000 stadia. Its length, width, and height are equal. Then he measured its wall, 144 cubits according to human measurement, which the angel used. (Rev. 21:15–17)

What John sees here is a vision of God's temple, specifically the Holy of Holies, descending from heaven to the earth. Perhaps you haven't recently measured a stadia or a cubit. Me either, but these figures are very important for understanding what the Bible is trying to show us. The cube that descends from heaven has a perimeter of roughly 5,500 miles, or roughly the perimeter of the known Hellenistic world at the time.

What does this mean? It means God's place is not only a garden of Eden. It is not only the land promised to God's people. Every square inch of the earth belongs to the King, and when He returns it will be evident that there is no place that does not belong to Him. "The earth and everything in it, the world and its inhabitants, belong to the Lord" (Ps. 24:1).

The kingdom does not belong in Jerusalem. The kingdom belongs in all the earth.

Jesus is not just King over Jerusalem. He is King over New York City. His lordship extends over the Sahara. He reigns and rules over the Himalayas and the Grand Canyon. He is King in Mexico and Manilla. He is sovereign in Tokyo and Cairo. Even the ground underneath your feet right now—all places and peoples belong to Him.

God's purposes will endure forever.

God's purpose from the beginning has been to extend His glory to all of creation. That's exactly how the story ends—all things acknowledging Christ as King by giving God alone praise.

We read in Revelation,

> I did not see a temple in it, because the Lord God the Almighty and the Lamb are its temple. The city does not need the sun or the moon to shine on it, because the glory of God illuminates it, and its lamp is the Lamb. The nations will walk by its light, and the kings of the earth will bring their glory into it. (21:22–24)

At the end of the story, Christ is front and center, receiving all glory and praise.

The nations see Him as the Son of a woman who has come to crush the head of the serpent. The peoples see that He is the Son of Abraham who came to offer a sacrifice that blesses all nations. He is vindicated as the Son of David whose kingdom has no end.

Since the beginning of creation, people have been dependent upon the sun and the moon for light, governing both the day and the night. But in this new creation kingdom, we will have no need for them anymore because Christ is our light. He is the true image-bearer who has extended the glory of God and the light of His kingdom to all peoples.

John continues,

> The throne of God and of the Lamb will be in the city, and his servants will worship him. They will see his face, and his name will be

> on their foreheads. Night will be no more; people will not need the light of a lamp or the light of the sun, because the Lord God will give them light, and they will reign forever and ever. (22:3–5)

What we are seeing here at the end of the story is not just a return to Eden, but something so much better. All of God's purposes for humanity that were given to Adam and Eve have been completed by Christ.

At the end of this story, we see that Christ's kingdom has been established forever.

Remember and Rehearse

Remember the ending.

The beautiful ending of the Christian story is an invitation to no longer live in the false or disorienting stories of our world. There is no better story than the King bringing His kingdom, because when the King brings His kingdom, He will raise the dead; He will judge all evildoers; He will enact perfect justice; and He will grant everlasting life to all who believe in Him.

An understandable response to the wonderful news of the coming kingdom is, "How long, Lord?" In the midst of the brokenness of the world, our souls groan for all things to be made new. As we long for the coming kingdom, we remember that the one who was faithful to come in Christ will be faithful to come again. When we long for the second coming of Christ, remember the first coming of Christ.

Rehearse the good news of Christ's coming kingdom by living faithfully today.

Specifically, we rehearse the coming kingdom when we live toward the kingdom in the present. In other words, we are invited to live now how we will live then. As citizens of the kingdom of heaven, we are called to live faithfully in the present in the same way we will live in future.

Because the King is bringing His kingdom, we have the opportunity to participate in a story that we do not write. We are invited to live in the story that Jesus Christ is writing and will one day finish. The doctrine of end times tells us that we have the opportunity to bind our stories together with the story of Jesus Christ.

The ending of the Christian story is an invitation to live in the true story of the kingdom of God. The ending of this story helps us to no longer be blinded by the light of the false stories of the world, but to live according to the truth that our King is coming to us.

The end reminds us of our justification. If you have placed your faith in Christ, your name is written in the Book of Life. One day you will stand before the judgment seat of Christ and He will declare you righteous. Not because of anything you have done, but because He credits His account to you.

The end of the story fuels our sanctification. One day, by the grace of God, we will be made perfectly holy. Because one day we will be completely holy, we can confidently walk in holiness today.

The end of the story is not just about the future. It's about learning how to bring the future into the present. The gift of the end of the storyline of Scripture is that we live with confidence today knowing what our future holds. We are one day closer to the King bringing His kingdom. That should bring joyful anticipation into the heart of every Christian. Our King is coming to us. He will bring His kingdom with Him. His reign and rule will have no end.

We will be His people.

There will be no more grief, sorrow, or crying. He will wipe away every last tear.

Death will be defeated.

The brokenness of this world will finally pass away.

We love the kingdom of God, not just because of all the benefits of kingdom citizenship, but because we love the King and we can't wait to see Him face-to-face.

The ending of the Christian story gives us the ultimate hope that one day God's will will be done on earth as it is in heaven. We will see the King. He will look us in the eyes. He will embrace us. He will wipe away all our tears and the former things will fade into the past.

Our story began with, "In the beginning, God." Our story ends with Him saying, "I am coming soon."

Until that day, we are invited to pray according to the grain of Scripture, "Come, Lord Jesus!" (Rev. 22:20). "Your kingdom come. Your will be done on earth as it is in heaven" (Matt. 6:10).

Amen.

Summary

The story of Scripture ends with God's kingdom established on earth forever. His presence is finally and forever in the midst of His people, and they are free to live out His purposes in His place.

Discussion Questions

1. How would you tell the ending of the story of the kingdom of God?

2. Who is one person specifically that you plan on sharing the story with?

3. What loose ends from the biblical story did you see tied together in this final chapter?

4. How does the truth about the end times give you hope for today?

Formation Exercise: The Christian Story

Now that you have an understanding of the full storyline of Scripture, practice telling that story conversationally over the course of 15–20 minutes, by using the framework of the kingdom of God—presence, people, purpose, and place. Continue to practice this over the following weeks and months, asking God to give you opportunities to share it with those who do not yet know Him.

About the Author

J. T. English PhD, serves as a pastor, a professor, and is the author of *Deep Discipleship: How the Local Church Can Make Whole Disciples*. J. T. is passionate about seeing God glorified through discipleship in the context of the local church.

He is also a cofounder of Training the Church, a ministry focused on assisting churches and ministry leaders develop sustainable discipleship framework for their context. He is also cohost for *Knowing Faith*, a podcast that explores basic Christian beliefs. He received his ThM in Historical Theology from Dallas Theological Seminary and PhD in Systematic Theology from Southern Seminary.

Acknowledgments

Thank you to Erik Wolgemuth for his help navigating the publishing world and his desire to help make discipleship resources available to the church.

Thank you to Devin Maddox, Mary Wiley, Kim Stanford, Whitney Alexander, and the entire B&H Publishing Team at Lifeway. I'm so thankful for a team that shares a vision of creating helpful resources for the church. I'm so thankful for our long-standing partnership.

Thank you to the thousands of students who've heard me teach this material in the church. Your questions and interactions have not only made me a better teacher, but they've helped me understand the story of the Bible in deeper ways. I've loved doing theology with you.

Finally, I'd like to thank my family, Macy, Thomas, and Bailey. There's just no way a project like this would ever see the light of day without your love and support. You've heard me talk about the ideas in this book around the dinner table far before they made it onto a page. I love each of you so much.

Notes

1. Richard Kearney, *On Stories* (London: Routledge, 2001), 31.

2. Alasdair MacIntyre, *After Virtue: A Study in Moral Theory*, 3rd ed. (Notre Dame, IN: University of Notre Dame Press, 2007), 251.

3. John Calvin, *Calvin: Institutes of the Christian Religion*, trans. Ford Lewis Battles, vol. 1 (Louisville, KY: Westminster John Knox, 2001).

4. "The State of Theology," The State of Theology, accessed December 23, 2023, https://thestateoftheology.com.

5. Craig G. Bartholomew and Michael W. Goheen, *The Drama of Scripture: Finding Our Place in the Biblical Story* (Grand Rapids: Baker, 2014), 31.

6. Jen Wilkin, *In His Image: 10 Ways God Calls Us to Reflect His Character* (Wheaton, IL: Crossway, 2018).

7. T. Desmond Alexander, *From Paradise to the Promised Land: An Introduction to the Pentateuch* (Grand Rapids: Baker Academic, 2012), 126.

8. Stephen G. Dempster, *Dominion and Dynasty: A Biblical Theology of the Hebrew Bible* (Downers Grove, IL: IVP Academic, 2003), 59.

9. Craig G. Bartholomew, *Where Mortals Dwell: A Christian View of Place for Today*, Illustrated edition (Grand Rapids: Baker Academic, 2011), 13.

10. For an in-depth consideration of kingdom and covenant, see Peter J. Gentry and Stephen J. Wellum, *Kingdom through Covenant: A Biblical-Theological Understanding of the Covenants* (Wheaton, IL: Crossway, 2012).

11. Jen Wilkin, *Ten Words to Live By: Delighting in and Doing What God Commands* (Wheaton, IL: Crossway, 2021).

12. The new covenant is referred to in different ways by different authors. It is referred to as the Everlasting Covenant: Jeremiah 32:36–41; 50:2–5; Ezekiel 16:59–63; 37:15–28; Isaiah 55:1–5; 61:8–9, the Covenant of Peace: Isaiah 54:1–10; Ezekiel: 34:20–31, and a promise of a new heart and spirit: Ezekiel 11:18–21; 18:30–32; Isaiah 59:21, but the message remains the same, God is going to bring His kingdom to earth.